PROBLEMS AND PRACTICES OF DEVELOPMENT BANKS

Problems and Practices of
DEVELOPMENT BANKS

by Shirley Boskey

published for The International Bank for
Reconstruction and Development

by The Johns Hopkins Press, Baltimore

Foreword

DEVELOPMENT BANKS ARE ENJOYING a growing popularity as instruments of economic development in the industrialized and less-developed countries alike. There are some eighty such institutions in the less-developed countries which are members of the International Bank; several of these countries have a number of development banks. The International Bank has provided financial support and technical advice for several recently created banks, and member countries have been asking with increasing frequency for assistance in establishing new institutions and for advice concerning the operations of existing ones.

As it responded to these requests, the Bank became aware of the paucity of information generally available on the experience of development banks. Moreover, it became apparent that neither the sponsors of new development banks nor the management of existing banks had much opportunity to study and benefit from the example of operations elsewhere.

The first effort on the part of the Bank to provide general practical guidance in the development bank field took the form of a book entitled *Development Banks,* written by William Diamond, a member of the staff of the Bank. This considered the purposes which may be served by a development bank, the conditions affecting private investment with which such a bank is designed to deal, and the experience of advanced countries in financing industry. It also discussed some of the problems and choices faced in forming and operating a development bank.

Next, the Bank invited executive officers of development banks in twelve countries to attend a week-long conference in Washington during May 1958. Participants were associated with banks in Brazil, Ceylon, Chile, France, India, Mexico, Pakistan, Puerto Rico, South Africa, Turkey, the United Kingdom and the United States. The International Finance Corporation was also represented.

The conference had two principal objectives. One was to provide an opportunity for development bank managers to talk over common problems and to learn how those problems were being dealt with by institutions in other countries. The other objective was to add to the Bank's own knowledge and understanding of the problems which confront development banks.

The institutions whose officials participated in the conference were diverse in economic environment, operating policies and scope of activity. Both government banks and banks under private management and control were represented. The discussions made clear, however, that despite this diversity and some consequent differences in approach to particular problems, there was a striking degree of agreement about what constituted the most perplexing operational problems for a development bank manager. Moreover, the solutions devised by one bank often seemed appropriate, with slight modification, for use by other, superficially quite different banks. The possibility that still other institutions might find in these solutions something of value for their operations suggested the desirability of wide dissemination of the experience of the banks represented at the conference, through a publication based upon the conference discussions.

Such is the origin of this book. The author is a member of the Bank's Technical Assistance and Liaison Staff, which has broad responsibilities for the International Bank's activities in the development bank field. She served as secretary of the development bank conference. Mr. Mervyn L. Weiner, a member of the Bank's Department of Operations—Western Hemisphere, was assigned for several months to assist in preparing the first draft of the manuscript.

The book does not purport to be an official statement of the views or policies of the International Bank. However, it is hoped that it will prove a useful and effective guide to those concerned with the theory and practice of development banks.

Richard H. Demuth, DIRECTOR
TECHNICAL ASSISTANCE AND LIAISON STAFF

Preface

A FEW COMMENTS CONCERNING the scope and structure of this book may be helpful to the reader.

The book is intended to be read as a companion to the earlier *Development Banks,* by William Diamond. Some of the ground covered by that book is necessarily gone over again here, but duplication has been kept to a minimum. The factors relevant in considering whether a development bank should be created are not dealt with; for these, Mr. Diamond's book should be consulted. The text is based largely upon the development bank conference discussions; these have been supplemented by drawing on documents and on studies of other institutions available in the International Bank.

Development banks may function in the agricultural as well as the industrial field. As used in this book, however, the term "development bank" refers to institutions, public or private, which have as one of their principal functions the making of medium- or long-term investments in industrial projects.

There are at present relatively few development banks which are owned wholly or principally by private interests and which are under private control and management. But there is a lively, widespread and growing interest in the potential of this type of institution. This has seemed to justify devoting considerable attention to some of the problems peculiar to private banks, notwithstanding that the number of such institutions is as yet small in relation to the number of public banks and their operating experience rather brief.

The book is divided into two parts. The first discusses the principal problems which confront the sponsors of a new bank, and notes some ways of dealing with them. The second part discusses the principal issues which arise in day-to-day operations, and some of the ways in which these issues have been resolved. While the considerations pointing to one or another solution are indicated, an effort has been made to avoid advocating any single approach to a particular problem. To the extent that judgments are expressed, they should be taken as the opinions of the author and not as an official statement of the policies of the International Bank.

The Appendix contains reference material in the form of selected charter provisions, policy statements, standard clauses of agreements, etc., of several development banks. This material is intended to supplement the analytical discussion in the text, and to illustrate a variety of ways of designing formal documents to meet particular demands of law or circumstance. There is also included a list of development banks in the less-developed member countries of the International Bank, indicating the kind of financing each institution offers. This information is intended primarily as a guide to investors and industrialists contemplating a direct approach to a development bank for financial assistance.

THE TEXT OF THIS BOOK reflects the comments and suggestions of many persons, within and outside the Bank, whose assistance is gratefully acknowledged.

Participants in the development bank conference not only provided much of the source material through their lively and informative discussions, but also kindly undertook to review references to their institutions and to supply recent data. Mr. Richard H. Demuth, whose idea it was that this book should and could be written, did not shirk the consequence of critically and patiently reading and talking over all drafts of the manuscript, and made many specific suggestions for its improvement. Mr. Mervyn L. Weiner contributed the first drafts for three of the chapters before taking up his post as a member of the Bank's resident mission in Peru. Messrs. Michael L. Hoffman and William Diamond offered detailed and sound criticism of substance and presentation; Mr. Diamond generously drew upon his extensive first-hand knowledge of the practice of development banking. Other Bank staff members gave of their time and thoughts, often beyond the demands of official duty; their help is appreciated no less for being here acknowledged collectively.

Shirley Boskey

Contents

Part II—Problems of Operation

PART I

Problems of Establishment

CHAPTER I

Purposes and Types
of Development Banks

THIS BOOK IS CONCERNED with a relatively new kind of investment institution. Institutions established principally or solely to provide long-term financing for industry have long been known.[1] The development bank, intended not only to provide capital for the private industrial sector, but also to mobilize savings, enterprise and skills for productive investment in that sector, is largely a post-World War II creation.

The last fifteen years have seen the less-developed countries swept by a determination to accelerate the pace of their economic development. This determination has been manifested by an increasing emphasis on industrialization, and by the hope that industrial expansion can be speedily achieved.

However, progress has been impeded in most countries by the lack or inadequacy of various ingredients of industrial development. The first impediment is a shortage of capital for industrial investment. In the more advanced countries industrial expansion was achieved in large part through self-financing and, in the early stages of industrialization, at a slow pace. The less-developed countries, spurred by the rapidity of their political advancement during recent years, feel it a necessity to achieve their economic growth at a faster pace. But their resources do not permit the accumulation of earnings sufficient to finance a rate of growth satisfactory to them. Some capital usually

---

[1] See William Diamond, *Development Banks,* The Johns Hopkins Press, 1957, pp. 19-40.

does exist in the form of private savings but not enough, and only a small part of those savings is in any event readily available for investment in industry; wealth is traditionally invested in land or commercial enterprises.

The second ingredient of industrial development which is generally lacking is an effective mechanism for channeling into productive investment a sufficiently large proportion of such savings as exist. The absence of a capital market means in turn that there is little familiarity with investment financing techniques. Finally, many countries suffer from a limited initiative on the part of the industrial community—a disinclination to seek out and to venture into new areas of activity—and from limited or no opportunity to become acquainted with and to profit by technological advances achieved abroad.

To help in overcoming these obstacles and in supplying the missing ingredients, the institution known as a development bank has been devised. Some eighty are now functioning all over the world in the less-developed countries which are members of the International Bank.

A number of these banks have been established with the assistance of the International Bank, and in some cases the Bank has provided the foreign exchange needed for their operations.

A principal reason for the International Bank's original interest in development banks was that they offered a practical solution to the difficulties the Bank encountered in financing small private industrial projects directly. Where the projects were many and the amounts sought were small, the Bank could not afford to undertake the detailed technical and creditworthiness appraisals which are a normal preliminary to a loan. Moreover, effective appraisal of such projects called for a greater knowledge of local conditions and the business standing of the sponsors than the Bank possessed or could readily acquire. More important, it was not feasible for most private enterprises to obtain, and many were reluctant to accept, the government guarantee required by the Bank's charter when a loan is made to a non-governmental borrower. However, these difficulties were avoided or surmounted when the borrower was a local financial institution, which could readily obtain a government guarantee, could select the most promising enterprises for financing out of the proceeds of the Bank's loan, and could undertake the necessary technical and financial appraisals.

Considerations such as these accounted for the initial appeal of development banks as vehicles for International Bank assistance to private industry. Experience has furnished broader grounds. The success of these institutions in stimulating new investment in and by the private industrial sector, and in making available new skills and enterprise as well as capital, has proved their value as instruments of economic development in their own right.

Because each bank is a response to the particular needs of the country which it serves, and to the political, economic and social environment in which it functions, there is considerable variety among them, particularly in scope of activity.

Most are public institutions, owned and managed by the government. Several are owned jointly by government and private capital, the latter generally having a minority interest. A few are privately owned and controlled.

Some development banks play a major role as financing institutions; for others, providing finance is of less significance. A few are a source of capital for government undertakings as well as for the private sector. Most assist industrial enterprises exclusively; some will also finance large-scale commercial agriculture, or agricultural undertakings integrated with a manufacturing operation. Within the industrial sector, normally only manufacturing or processing enterprises are eligible for assistance, but a few banks are prepared to finance service industries or housing projects. Many concentrate on medium- and large-scale industry; some have been created expressly to cater to the needs of small enterprises.

Most banks are free to provide funds in whatever way seems most appropriate: by equity participations, or loans, or some intermediate form of investment. Some, however, are not authorized to invest in shares.

Many development banks provide their clients with various kinds of technical assistance—engineering, accounting or management advice—on projects they finance; some will advise on a project even if they are not financing it. Other institutions offer no technical assistance, even to clients, beyond that incident to effective administration of their investment.

Some banks investigate promising new investment opportunities, bringing them to the attention of private businessmen. Many of these banks enter the industrial arena directly, establishing enterprises and arranging for their operation until such time as private capital can be induced to take them over.

Some banks engage in activities designed to promote a capital market, actively seeking to broaden the base of industrial ownership by selling investments from their portfolios, by underwriting industrial issues, or, more indirectly, by issuing their own securities.

A few banks have been made responsible for general economic programming for the country.

This great variety among existing banks indicates that no single model is suitable to all, perhaps not even to any two, countries. The design of the bank must be drawn in the light of its purposes and of the economic, social and political environment in which it is to function.

Thus the first group of issues confronting the sponsors of a new bank has to do with the bank's purposes. Is it to be only a financial institution? Is it to offer extensive technical assistance services, or engage in promotional activities, doing research or establishing industries itself? Will it provide only loan funds, or risk capital as well? Is it to concentrate on large and medium-scale enterprises, or on small concerns, or is its assistance to be given without regard to the size of the enterprise? The answers to these and related questions are important in determining not only the design of the bank, but also whether it must be a government institution or can be established with private capital.

In some situations government finance and direction are obviously called for: for example, where the bank is to operate entirely in the public sector, channeling public funds to public enterprises or executing and operating public projects such as highway construction, power development or public works.

But even where the object is assistance to the private sector, it may not always be possible to attract private capital to the bank without an unreasonable degree of government subsidy. This is likely to be the case, for example, where the primary objective is to provide finance for enterprises which are pioneering and promotional in character. Enterprises of this type may be expected to prove profitable in the long run, but are not likely to show returns soon enough or large enough to be considered satisfactory by private shareholders. Moreover, because there are likely to be other more immediately attractive investment opportunities, private investors would probably be reluctant to assume the risk that the experimental ventures might never be profitable. A public institution can more easily await delayed returns from new industries, and it is in a better position to keep an enterprise going for other than investment considerations.

It may also be difficult to induce private investors to subscribe to the equity of a bank intended to cater primarily to the long-term capital needs of small enterprises, which normally have little industrial experience and frequently are one-man ventures. This type of financing is inherently risky, and it is difficult for the development bank to arrange to invest on terms which would compensate it for the risk. For reasons discussed later in this book, the bank will probably find that its financing must take the form of loans. An institution which is to engage primarily in loan financing, and whose borrowers will be numerous and small, can look forward on the one hand to high costs of investigation and administration, and on the other hand to returns not only fixed but relatively small. Here again there is a case for a public institution. Being free, as they usually are, from pressure to make large profits, public banks can contemplate with greater equanimity the prospect of fixed and low returns, and can more readily assume the administrative costs of many small loans to small clients.

Where the environment is inflationary and the demand is for long-term credits, it may likewise be difficult to establish a private bank. Owners of capital hesitate to lend directly at long-term when the value of money is declining, and may therefore not be willing to do so indirectly, by investing in the equity of an institution whose principal activity will be providing loan capital.[2]

If, on the other hand, the purposes of the bank and the environ-

---

[2] Investment in the bank's shares will have a greater appeal if they offer an opportunity to hedge against inflation—that is, where it is contemplated that the bank will make index-bound loans, or loans with a gold or dollar clause, or will invest heavily in industrial equities.

ment in which it is to function are such that it appears feasible to organize a privately-owned and managed institution, there are substantial advantages in doing so. Experience indicates that in appropriate circumstances, a private development bank, properly organized and staffed, can be a particularly effective mechanism for promoting industrial growth.

It should be recognized at the outset that a private bank normally cannot be established on a sound financial basis unless the government is prepared to extend generous financial support. Returns satisfactory to private shareholders cannot be expected in the absence of substantial government financing on terms which make that assistance in essence a subsidy. But the fact that the private institution is not part of the machinery of government, and that its management is selected by and responsible to private shareholders, means that it will in many cases be better able than a public institution to make investment decisions objectively, without being subject to political pressures. Moreover, as compared with a public bank, a private institution is likely to have considerable freedom to engage and dismiss staff, and to establish administrative and fiscal procedures appropriate to its purposes and needs. The ability thus to function on a businesslike and efficient basis will in turn increase the bank's effectiveness in stimulating investment activity in the private industrial sector.

It would, of course, be wrong to suggest either that public banks are necessarily susceptible to political influence or that private banks are necessarily immune to any kind of influence. It would be equally unfair to suggest that a public bank cannot, by its nature, be efficient.

Many public banks have achieved a high degree of independence of the government proper. But the closer the link to government through ownership and management, the greater the likelihood of government influence on investment decisions.

Similarly, there are some highly efficient public banks. The experience of a number of others suggests that accountability to the head of a government department or to the legislature may be less effective in keeping an agency up to the mark than a responsibility owed to private shareholders. If a government enterprise consistently operates at a loss it may well become the subject of a legislative inquiry, but should it merely be less profitable than was expected, it may function undisturbed for years. The shareholders in a private enterprise, on the other hand, insist upon a satisfactory return on their investment, and they also expect the investment itself to increase in value. For a private development bank, this means not only that investments must be sound but that the institution itself must be efficiently and economically operated.

It has already been noted that there are only a few development banks in which the entire share capital, or a majority interest, is in private hands, and which are under private control and management. But the number of such banks has been increasing steadily. In July 1959, there were six in active operation in the less-developed countries which are members of the International Bank: the Industrial Development Bank of Turkey, the Industrial Credit and Investment Corporation of India, the Development Finance Corporation of Ceylon, the Agricultural Industrial and Real Estate Credit Bank of Lebanon, the Pakistan Industrial Credit and Investment Corporation, and the Industrial Finance Corporation of South Africa. The Industrial Development Bank of Israel is under private control, although its initial capital has come largely from public sources.

Several other private banks have recently been established or are expected to come into being soon. The China Development Corporation, organized in the spring of 1959 (but not yet in operation), is under private control, although the government is a shareholder. Another "mixed" bank under private management has just been established in the Federation of Malaya. The Industrial and Mining Development Bank of Iran opened its doors in October 1959. A privately-owned development bank was established in Thailand in late 1959 as successor to a government institution. Announcement has been made of a development bank for the Northern Region (Syria) of the United Arab Republic, with 69% of the shares being offered for public subscription. The National Investment Corporation of Tunisia, established in April 1959 with the government holding a majority of the shares, plans to increase its capital and is inviting subscriptions by small private shareholders; if the offering is fully taken up, the government will become a minority shareholder. A proposal to reorganize a government bank in Peru, to bring in private share capital and to place control in private hands, has been accepted in principle by the government. In several other countries, plans for private development banks are under active and serious consideration.

It was this evidence of the growing popularity of the private development bank as a vehicle for stimulating industrial development that led the International Bank to believe that it would be useful to set forth in this book in some detail the experience of existing private banks.

CHAPTER II

Establishing a Development Bank—Some Initial Problems

MANY ISSUES REMAIN to be resolved after the bank's purposes have been determined and the decision whether to create a public or private institution has been made. The next three chapters, which form the balance of Part I of this book, deal with other questions to be taken into account in planning the design of the bank. Chapter III considers various aspects of the institution's finances, such as the desirable magnitude of its resources, its capital structure and possible sources of share capital and borrowed funds. The board of directors and the relationship between the board and management are the subjects of Chapter IV. The present chapter addresses itself to another group of issues, relating to incorporation of the bank, the drafting of the bank's charter and the recruitment of top management.

Method of Incorporation

A government-financed and managed bank will normally be created by the legislature or by executive decree. A private institution may be established either pursuant to the general corporation laws of the country or by special statute. Most of the private banks have been established under the general corporation laws. However, the Development Finance Corporation of Ceylon and the Industrial Finance Corporation of Thailand were created by act of the legislature. Among other reasons for this course of action, the evidence of government sponsorship provided by the statute was thought likely to give potential private investors greater confidence in the bank's shares. (The two governments disavowed any intention to seek to control or influence management.)

Incorporation under the general corporation laws may be considered more compatible with the bank's private character than incorporation by special statute. Moreover, it may be thought that legislative participation in the creation of the bank will encourage too active an interest by the government in the bank's affairs. It is doubtful, however, that there is any necessary relationship between the method of incorporation and the degree of freedom from government interference. The institution's independence is more likely to depend upon the soundness and independence of its management than upon the technique of incorporation or the form of constituent documents.

The choice of one or the other methods of incorporation is likely to have practical significance for the bank only insofar as it affects the ease with which the charter may be amended and the extent of the shareholders' control over amendments. A charter framed under the general corporation laws may be amended by the shareholders. But where a special statute serves as the charter, amendment may be accomplished only by the legislature, and the legislature may act without regard to or in disregard of the wishes of the shareholders. The latter can of course propose amendments, but the legislature may not be willing to adopt them. In any event, amendment of a special statute is likely to be a more time-consuming process than amendment of a corporate charter.

Even where the institution is created under the general corporation laws, however, special legislative action may be called for. Certain provisions of those laws may be incompatible with the purposes of the bank or may impose onerous or inappropriate limitations or responsibilities upon it, and special legislation will be required if the bank is to be exempted from these provisions. Or the government may be prepared to give the bank privileges to which it would not be entitled under the general corporation laws. For example, the Industrial Development Bank of Turkey, although incorporated as a joint stock company, was by special statute exempted from the general banking laws of Turkey and certain provisions of the commercial code which would have unduly restricted its borrowing power.[1]

Drafting the Charter

Precision of Charter Language. Many provisions of a charter are customarily set forth in language as precise and unequivocal as possible—those relating to capital structure and to the composition of the board of directors, for example. But other provisions may be phrased generally or specifically. Thus the policies and activities of some banks are specified and delimited by their charters, while for others considerable discretion in these areas is left to the board of directors. The sponsors must decide where to use general language and where to be specific.

General language has the obvious advantage of giving the board of directors maximum freedom to fashion policy and to adapt the bank's activities or the emphasis of its operations to changing circumstances. Specific language, on the other hand, can provide the directors with a welcome defense against political or shareholder pressure and with a measure of immunity from criticism of policies. Charter provisions which limit the exercise of the board's discretion by confining the bank's activities to particular fields or geographic areas, which prescribe an order of priority among economic sectors, or which direct that applications be considered solely on their economic and technical merits have sometimes proved useful in this respect; so have specific provisions concerning dividend and reserve policies, described later in this chapter.

Some charters combine a measure of restriction with a measure of flexibility. For example, the Banco Nacional do Desenvolvimento Economico of Brazil may operate only in fields specified by its charter. Some are described narrowly, as e.g., "electric power" and "railway transport." But it may also function in the field of "basic industries," and it is for the bank to decide what industries are "basic" at any given time. Flexibility can also be achieved by delib-

---

[1] By the special statute, the government also guaranteed a minimum dividend.

erately failing to deal with certain matters in the charter, leaving them to regulations adopted by the bank. Such a technique is especially useful where the bank is created by special statute, in view of the possible delays and difficulties of the amendment process. It was followed in the case of the Development Finance Corporation of Ceylon. The directors adopted regulations in the first instance; these are subject to amendment by special resolution of the shareholders.

Another approach is to arrange for the early adoption by the directors of a statement of policy, omitting from the charter specific provisions bearing on the issues to be covered by the policy statement. This was done in the case of the Industrial Credit and Investment Corporation of India and the Pakistan Industrial Credit and Investment Corporation, created under the general corporation laws.[2]

Definitions. Experience suggests that the bank may encounter difficulties if it is authorized to finance "private industrial" enterprises without some indication in the charter of the scope of those terms. Under some systems of law, directors of a corporation are personally liable for losses suffered by the corporation as a consequence of an *ultra vires* action. Where such was the rule of law and a client enterprise failed, causing a loss to the bank, the directors might be personally liable upon a judicial determination that the bank was not empowered to finance that kind of enterprise.

The Development Finance Corporation of Ceylon began its operations under a charter which authorized it to finance "private" enterprises without defining the term "private." A question arose as to its authority to assist enterprises in which the government had a financial interest. Fearing that assistance to such enterprises might be held *ultra vires,* not being expressly authorized by the charter, the directors decided to reject applications from any concern in which the government had an interest, however nominal. Since many companies had sought government financing to become eligible for a special income tax exemption, this decision disqualified numerous otherwise meritorious applicants for assistance. To resolve the dilemma, the legislature amended the charter to include within the

[2] See Appendix C for the text of the statement adopted by the latter; that adopted by the Indian bank is almost identical.

category of "private" enterprises any enterprise in which no more than 20% of the capital is held by the government.

Other charters are less specific on the point. Under the charter of the Pakistan Industrial Credit and Investment Corporation, a nominal government share participation or loan does not by itself withdraw an enterprise from the private sector, if the enterprise is privately operated and managed and the government's interest is neither directly nor indirectly controlling. The charter of the International Finance Corporation, after stating the Corporation's objective to be the financing of private enterprise in association with private investors, declares that the existence of a government or other public interest in an enterprise shall not necessarily preclude an investment by the Corporation.[3]

The issue of definition also arises where the development bank is authorized to assist "industrial" enterprises. There is general agreement that the term encompasses manufacturing or processing enterprises. But there has sometimes been a question whether the term "industrial" is broad enough to cover private shipping or other transportation ventures, hotels, site clearing and construction companies, or commercial agriculture operations. Where the bank is intended to have the broadest possible authority, the difficulty may be avoided by a charter provision authorizing assistance to "productive" enterprise, with an indication in the charter or in a statement of policy, such as described above, that it is expected that the emphasis of financing will be on industrial enterprises.[4] If, on the other hand, it is intended not to authorize assistance to certain kinds of enterprises which might reasonably be held to be industrial in character (e.g., large-scale agricultural undertakings, which have many of the characteristics of industrial enterprise), it would seem advisable to exclude these explicitly.

Reserve Provisions. Ordinary prudence leads banks to establish

[3] See Chapter V, Selection of Enterprises, for discussion of the practice of these institutions under such charter provisions.

[4] This procedure was followed in the case of the International Finance Corporation. The charter refers only to "productive" enterprises. An explanatory memorandum on the draft charter submitted to governments for approval, and the booklets which describe the Corporation's actual investment policies, make it clear that the Corporation will finance enterprises which are predominantly industrial.

reserves adequate to meet all their obligations. But an explicit charter directive can provide the board of directors with a refuge against shareholder pressure for dividends before reserves have accumulated to a point the board considers satisfactory.

This may be an important consideration for a private bank. Several such institutions are required by their charters (which in some cases reflect applicable provisions of the country's general corporation laws) to transfer to reserves a specified percentage of profits, until reserves equal a stated proportion of paid-in capital, or of debt outstanding, or of loans made. The Industrial Development Bank of Turkey must set aside 5% of profits as a "legal reserve fund." The Jordan Development Bank must place 15% of net profits in a reserve. The Agricultural, Industrial and Real Estate Credit Bank of Lebanon must set aside 10% of net profit as a legal reserve, until reserves equal one-third of the bank's capital. The Industrial Credit and Investment Corporation of India is required each year, beginning five years after its incorporation, to set aside out of profits otherwise available for dividends a minimum of 25% of such profits for contingencies and purposes other than dividends, until reserves equal the amount of the government advance outstanding. Complicated reserve provisions were written into the charter of the Pakistan Industrial Credit and Investment Corporation.[5] The charter of the Development Finance Corporation of Ceylon requires that until the government advance is repaid, at least 20% of net profits shall be set aside annually in a special reserve fund until the fund equals the amount of the advance outstanding; these amounts may not be used for the business of the Corporation, but may be invested in "appropriate" securities.

Some charters direct the establishment of a separate reserve for bad debts, sometimes in terms of a specified sum to be set aside each year, sometimes in terms of a percentage of loans outstanding or of net profits. The Industrial Development Bank of Turkey, for example, must set aside 5% of net profits as a reserve against losses (additional to the 5% in the "legal reserve fund"). Even where there is no charter requirement, banks commonly establish reserves against losses as a matter of policy. Some do so by setting aside an

[5] See page 18, below.

arbitrary sum annually; others set aside a lump sum estimated to be adequate for the purpose, and do not add to the reserve unless and until it is in fact drawn upon.

Dividend Limitation. The charters of wholly publicly owned banks do not usually incorporate a dividend limitation. Often it is not contemplated that the government will receive dividends on its contribution, even where the contribution is in the form of a subscription to share capital.

On the other hand, a dividend limitation is often specified where the institution's equity is held jointly by the government and private interests or entirely by the latter.[6] One object of such a provision, similar to that of a reserve requirement, is to assure that the board is not compelled by shareholder pressure to allocate a disproportionate share of profits to dividends at the expense of reserves. Where the government has provided a substantial part of the bank's resources, the limitation has the further purpose of precluding an undue profit to the private shareholders through the use of public funds. The government may in fact make a dividend limitation a condition of its assistance, to protect itself from criticism for making public moneys available to a private institution on too favorable terms.

Dividend ceilings vary considerably. A limitation of $2\frac{1}{4}\%$ in the charter of the Industrial Finance Corporation of India, a "mixed" bank, is applicable until such time as government loans have been repaid and reserves are equal to paid-in capital; thereafter the ceiling will become 5%.[7] There is a 6% ceiling on dividends to private shareholders in the Industrial Bank of Peru. A 12% ceiling is specified by the charters of the Industrial Development Bank of Turkey and the Development Finance Corporation of Ceylon. In

[6] The charter of the Industrial Development Corporation of South Africa sets a ceiling of 8% on dividends, except as approved by the Governor-General of the Union of South Africa. The bank is wholly government-owned, but the charter authorizes the sale of all or any part of the government's interest.

[7] The government has guaranteed a $2\frac{1}{4}\%$ dividend, and has thus far been called upon under its guarantee seven times. (The dividend has been met without assistance four times and repayment of amounts advanced by the government has begun.) Pursuant to the bank's statutory charter, dividends accruing on shares held by the government and the Reserve Bank are not paid over, but are credited to a special reserve fund.

the case of the latter, the ceiling is effective only until the government advance is repaid. The Pakistan Industrial Credit and Investment Corporation may pay a dividend not exceeding 7% out of profits remaining after allocating not less than 15% of net profits to reserves. If any profits still remain, not less than 10% must be used as a second allocation to reserves. Out of any profits still remaining, a second dividend not exceeding 6% may be distributed. The Agricultural, Industrial and Real Estate Credit Bank of Lebanon may pay dividends of up to 6% out of net profits remaining after a required allocation to reserves; any excess of net profits is to be divided equally between the bank and the government.

A dividend ceiling may have the unintended consequence of discouraging private investment in the bank itself, particularly if it should hold the maximum return to shareholders below what they might expect to earn elsewhere. If the bank's shares are to compete effectively with other investment opportunities, the level of any dividend ceiling must take account of going rates of return on alternative investments. Moreover, if the environment is inflationary and progressive deterioration of the currency in terms of exchange value and purchasing power is likely, a dividend ceiling which appeared reasonable initially may in fact preclude the shareholders from receiving more than a very small return on the actual value of their subscriptions. In such a situation, it may be desirable to express any limitation adopted in terms other than a flat percentage. It was with all these considerations in mind that an International Bank mission on one occasion suggested the following formula for a dividend ceiling: up to a stated percentage per annum on the face value of the equity expressed in the national currency, or up to a lesser percentage per annum on the original value of the equity expressed in U.S. dollars at the time the equity is fully subscribed, and revalued in the national currency at the date the dividend is paid, whichever is the greater.

Recruitment of Management

The importance of a thoughtful analysis of the functions to be performed, and of the need so to draft charter provisions that the performance of those functions will not be hampered, has been emphasized. But however conscientiously these preliminaries have been complied with, they will not by themselves insure the bank's success, even in the most favorable of economic circumstances. Arrangements must be made for capable and experienced management. With competent management a bank may be successful notwithstanding inadequacies in the original concept of the institution or shortcomings of its charter. But no bank, however well conceived, can overcome the handicap of poor management.

The chief executive officer (who may carry the title of president, chairman, managing director or general manager) is the most important member of the management. In some of the smaller institutions, he constitutes the entire management. Normally the charter gives him responsibility for day-to-day operations under the policy guidance of the board of directors.

It is extremely difficult to find a good general manager for a new development bank, and it is not much easier to do so after the bank's reputation has been established. The position calls for experience in long-term industrial financing, combined with such personal characteristics as energy, imagination and tact, probity and an ability to withstand outside pressures in the exercise of professional judgment. There are not many persons with the requisite qualifications even in the industrialized countries, and far fewer elsewhere.

The International Bank has on several occasions been asked to help in recruiting the first general manager of a new development bank, and it has always undertaken to provide whatever assistance it could. On occasion the private shareholders, particularly the foreign investors, have offered their help. The foreign investor group in the Industrial and Mining Development Bank of Iran has itself undertaken responsibility for management during the first five years, coincident with the period during which the group will elect a majority of the board.

Two principal difficulties have been encountered in recruiting a general manager, quite apart from the shortage of qualified candidates. One is created by the need in many cases to look for a non-national: the implied recognition that no qualified national can be found is often politically unpalatable. Other things being equal, a local general manager is normally to be preferred to a foreign manager. But it may be impossible to find a qualified local national, particularly in a country which has had little or no experience in long-term industrial financing, or indeed in industry. Moreover, prospective private shareholders are inclined to be reluctant to commit themselves without satisfactory assurance that operations will be in good hands. Even local private investors may equate competence with imported talent at the start; and prospective foreign investors are still more likely to be of this view. The decision to engage a non-national may be politically difficult, especially for a government institution, but the International Bank has nevertheless urged that it be made where it appears to be in the interest of the development bank.

The second difficulty arises from the fact that a non-national must usually be offered remuneration substantially higher than that which attaches to most administrative positions in the country.[8] The salary level which he can command at home will very likely be high in relation to the salary scales of a less-developed country. Moreover, a man who has attained some rank in the career service of a financial or industrial enterprise will expect to be compensated for loss of both seniority and career security. Added to this may be tax considerations: the general manager's remuneration may be subject to tax at home as well as in the country of employment. The governments of some less-developed countries, recognizing the deterrent effect of the double tax burden, have granted tax exemption to key positions which they are particularly anxious to fill. If the position of general manager is not exempt, some adjustment in remuneration may well have to be made to take account of the tax situation.

The International Bank has urged development banks not to make compensation the principal factor in their employment decisions: an unwillingness to meet the legitimate salary demands of a qualified candidate and the selection of a less competent individual simply because he is prepared to accept a lower figure may well prove false

---

[8] The "Operational and Executive Personnel" program, a new part of the United Nations' technical assistance activities, may be helpful here; in appropriate cases this program may be prepared to contribute the difference between the local salary scale and what is necessary to recruit a competent foreign manager.

economy. A single wrong decision attributable to inexperience or poor judgment could cost a bank much more in trouble or actual monetary loss than the amount saved in the manager's remuneration.

CHAPTER III

The Bank's Finances

Capital Structure

Magnitude of Resources. The International Bank is often asked how large the resources of a development bank ought to be. There is no categorical answer to this question, no formula to determine the "proper" magnitude of a given bank's capitalization. The bank ought to have sufficient capital to enable it to make an impact on industrial development, and to earn enough for expenses, the accumulation of adequate reserves and, in the case of a private institution, payment of a satisfactory dividend. On the other hand, resources should not be so large that they greatly exceed what appears reasonably necessary for the fulfillment of the bank's purposes. Overcapitalization, in the sense of having a great deal more funds than are needed to do the job—whether this is providing finance and technical assistance or establishing industries—may give rise to strong pressure to do too much too early and too fast.

Whatever the desirable capitalization figure from the standpoint of the bank's effectiveness, the actual resources at its disposal will in the last analysis be determined by practical considerations. Where the bank is to be a public institution, account must be taken of the implications for the national budget, i.e., what can be afforded without resort to inflationary means of financing. When a private bank is in view, an estimate must be made of the amount of private savings that can be tapped.

Relationship between Debt and Equity. Later in this chapter there is reference to the fact that institutional subscribers to shares of a development bank are usually motivated by other than purely investment considerations. Nevertheless, it is generally necessary to assure them of at least a modest return on their investment, and non-institutional potential investors may have to be persuaded that the bank's shares offer prospects of returns comparable to those which could be expected on alternative investments.

It is noted in Chapter I that private development banks have had to be given special privileges—in most cases an opportunity to earn a profit on long-term, interest-free government advances. To the extent that share capital is supplemented by conventional loan funds, the earning power of the shares is further increased: the higher the proportion of borrowed funds to share capital, the greater the potential earning power of the latter. But if the portion of total resources to be put up by shareholders is too small, the possibility of obtaining further capital by way of loans may be prejudiced. Prospective lenders will not lend unless they are satisfied that there is a sufficiently large equity cushion to protect their interests. In any case, since the share capital stands behind the bank's obligations, it is to the interest of the shareholders that borrowings remain safely below the level at which a substantial loss on the bank's investments might cause a default and wipe out the equity.

Still other factors are relevant. Borrowed funds impose fixed charges.[1] Equity capital imposes no fixed charges, but at the same time it may be more costly in the long run. If the bank is a success, it is likely that a larger total sum will be paid out as dividends than would have been paid out as interest on an equal amount of loan capital obtained on conventional terms. To the extent of the difference, the amount of funds available for reinvestment—and new earnings—will be reduced.

These considerations have little significance for a wholly government-owned bank which is not under pressure to earn large profits

---

[1] Loans made to development banks by the International Bank and the United States Development Loan Fund, referred to later in this chapter, are in the form of a line of credit, interest being charged only on the amount withdrawn and outstanding from time to time.

for its shareholders and which looks to the government for all of its resources. But they may be important, even for a public bank, if it is contemplated that the bank may sometime wish to borrow from other sources, perhaps through issuance of its own obligations.

The relationship between debt and equity in the bank's capital structure also has implications for the bank's investment policies which should not be overlooked. In determining the proportion of its resources which it can prudently employ to purchase equities, the bank must be mindful of the need to have sufficient funds in liquid or readily realizable form to meet its fixed obligations. A bank capitalized heavily with borrowed funds would probably be reluctant to invest heavily in equities, and might even accept only the more conservative loan proposals. Therefore, it may be said that if it is the primary purpose of the bank to provide risk capital, the bank's own capitalization should not contemplate a relatively high proportion of loan capital. On the other hand, a preponderance of loan capital would not be inappropriate for a bank expected to make few or no equity investments.

Taken together, these considerations can translate into a variety of debt-equity ratios in practice. There is no single "correct" ratio. The International Bank suggested a 3:1 ratio for the banks in Turkey, India, Pakistan and Iran, which it helped to establish. To encourage subscriptions to an increase in share capital, the ratio for the Turkish bank was later raised to 4:1, after the bank had established itself as a going concern. A 3.51:1 ratio is prescribed in the second loan agreement between the Investment Credit Corporation of Austria and the International Bank. The government advances to the Industrial Credit and Investment Corporation of India, the Pakistan Industrial Credit and Investment Corporation, the Investment Credit Corporation of Austria and the Industrial and Mining Development Bank of Iran are considered to be equity for purposes of the debt-equity ratio: in the event of liquidation, the Indian, Pakistan and Austrian government advances would rank for repayment not only after debts but also after the share capital, while the Iranian government advance would rank *pari passu* with the share capital. Thus the banks have ample scope for borrowing.

The Industrial Development Bank of Canada, a public bank, and the Commonwealth Development Finance Company, a "mixed" bank, are also by charter subject to a 3:1 ratio. Another "mixed" bank, the Industrial Finance Corporation of India, may borrow up to ten times the amount of its paid-in capital and reserves. Unless the shareholders approve, outstanding borrowings of the Industrial Development Corporation of South Africa, a public institution, may not exceed three-fourths of the issued capital.

It may be noted that the actual debt-equity ratio may change substantially where the bank has borrowed abroad and the local currency is thereafter devalued. The value of the equity would be reduced in relation to the amount of the loan, and the safety of outstanding foreign debt may be imperiled.

Sources of Equity Capital

With respect to the financing of public banks (whether wholly government-owned or "mixed," with the government holding a majority interest), it suffices to note here only that what corresponds to the share capital of a private bank may, in the case of a public institution, be provided in various ways.

Funds may come as annual appropriations, or Treasury advances, or a lump sum allocation which may or may not take the form of a subscription to share capital. In Yugoslavia, publicly owned enterprises are required to contribute to the public development bank's lendable resources, annually, the equivalent of a fixed percentage of their assets. Certain tax proceeds are earmarked for the development bank, a technique followed in other countries as well. Financial and investment companies and insurance companies and stock exchanges in Mexico are required to subscribe to shares of the Nacional Financiera (in which the government holds a small majority) in amounts corresponding to a specified proportion of their capital and reserves.[2]

A number of issues relating to sources of share capital for private banks warrant discussion. Their equity has, of course, come principally or wholly from private sources; foreign as well as domestic

[2] In some other countries (e.g., Haiti), particular types of business entities are required to make compulsory loans to the development bank, or to deposit funds with it.

investors have subscribed. As noted earlier, governments have taken minority participations in a few banks. And some have received government assistance in a form which, while not conventional equity, is sufficiently similar to justify describing it together with subscriptions to shares.

Domestic. A private development bank may, in theory at least, look to two different groups of domestic private investors: institutional and individual. Commercial banks and insurance companies were initial subscribers to the capital of the Development Finance Corporation of Ceylon, the Industrial Credit and Investment Corporation of India, the Industrial Finance Corporation of India and the Pakistan Industrial Credit and Investment Corporation.[3] Institutional investors are usually motivated by patriotism and principle, on the one hand, and on the other by the belief that the bank will perform a useful function for the economy in general, and may in consequence be of more or less direct benefit to their particular business interests. On occasion institutional support has been forthcoming only after special inducements (tax concessions or a government-guaranteed dividend) or government pressure. Commercial banks, industrial firms and trade associations took up the entire initial share capital of the Industrial Development Bank of Turkey, but first it was necessary for the government to offer a guaranteed minimum dividend and, in the case of the commercial banks, to exercise some persuasion.

Individual investors are harder to attract than institutions. As noted in Chapter I, it is likely to be particularly difficult to attract individuals when the bank is to finance small or developmental projects or to lend in an inflationary economy. However, in some situations private capital may be more responsive: where other investment opportunities are not considerably more attractive; where, for lack or inadequacy of a market mechanism, the investor is not aware of other opportunities; or where the known alternatives are considered less safe than investment in the bank's shares. Government sponsorship may reassure the small saver. And even though private

---

[3] In some cases it has been necessary to enact special legislation to qualify the bank's shares for institutional investment.

investors may hold back at the start, they may in time become more cordial. There were no individual subscribers to the initial share capital of the Industrial Development Bank of Turkey, but a capital issue four years later was oversubscribed, and many of the subscribers were individuals.

Where it seems that an appeal to both investor groups may prove successful, there are several considerations to be weighed before approaching either. Operations are probably facilitated when a few institutional investors hold all the equity. As noted above, these subscribers are likely to have acted largely for non-investment considerations. The extent and immediacy of the bank's profitability are therefore not likely to be of principal concern to such shareholders. They will probably be content, in the main, if the bank appears to be serving its purpose and if they receive a reasonable dividend. The individual shareholder, in contrast, is more likely to have a lively interest in the yield and safety of his investment, and to be satisfied only if returns are substantial, prompt and regular. He will be inclined to be impatient with investment policies which do not achieve this result.

However, while there are advantages from the standpoint of administration in a few large institutional shareholders, such an arrangement may be politically unacceptable where substantial government aid is to be extended. The government may be severely criticized for supporting and helping to finance a private bank in which the equity is to be narrowly held within the business community or by other wealthy groups. Moreover, widespread ownership achieved through a public offering of shares can engender widespread interest in, and support of, the bank's activities. This may be particularly helpful in the years during which the bank will be a pioneering institution, engaged in a kind of financing new or little known in the country.

When the Industrial Credit and Investment Corporation of India was established, an effort was made to reconcile these conflicting considerations by allocating 40% of the shares for private placement with large industrial groups and financial institutions within India, at the same time reserving 30% for individual investors. More than half the applications received for the public offering were for fewer than 20 shares.[4] The balance of 30% was allocated to foreign institutional investors. Similarly, 60% of the initial issue of shares of the Pakistan Industrial Credit and Investment Corporation was sold in Pakistan, one-third by public offering and the rest by private placement with banks, insurance companies and leading industrialists.[5]

Widespread share ownership has sometimes been advocated as a solution to the problem of how to prevent any single group of shareholders from acquiring voting control. It must be recognized, however, that even if shares are widely offered at the start, it is difficult to prevent a subsequent concentration of voting power. To attempt to do so by charter provisions (for example, by limiting the number of shares which one person may hold or by reducing voting rights per share as an individual's shareholdings increase) may adversely affect the marketability of shares. Moreover, formal restrictions would not hinder groups of individuals from coming together for the purpose of acquiring control. Recognizing this difficulty, the Industrial Credit and Investment Corporation of India and the Pakistan Industrial Credit and Investment Corporation agreed, as a condition of receiving government advances, that their directors' powers with respect to registration of share transfers would be so exercised as to prevent "any one person or company or group of affiliated persons or companies" from acquiring effective control.

Foreign. Foreign capital participation offers a development bank a number of possible advantages. It may help to insulate management against local political pressures to make or decline to make particular investments, thereby strengthening the bank's independence. It may promote a flow of external capital to local industry and provide a point of contact with capital markets in the industrialized countries. It may facilitate the importation of technical skills in industrial production and management. Finally, the evidence that overseas capital regards the bank's shares as a good risk may give

[4] The shares were of Rs. 100 each (U.S. $21 equivalent), at par.

[5] In May 1959 PICIC had 675 shareholders, all but 56 being Pakistani nationals. Domestic shareholders consisted of 383 private individuals, 203 industrialists and businessmen, 9 banks, 8 insurance companies and 16 business houses and other institutions.

confidence to potential domestic investors and lead them to invest their own funds.

Foreign banks and insurance companies doing business in the country are likely shareholder prospects. Being an integral part of the economy they, like their domestic counterparts, are often disposed to participate for other than purely investment reasons. Their subscriptions are usually facilitated by the fact that they can pay for their shares in local currency. British, Indian and Pakistani banks and British and Canadian insurance companies were among the initial subscribers to the capital of the Development Finance Corporation of Ceylon. British banks and insurance companies subscribed to shares of the Pakistan Industrial Credit and Investment Corporation and the Industrial Credit and Investment Corporation of India. Among the 13 commercial banks which subscribed to the initial share capital of the Industrial Development Bank of Turkey were several foreign banks doing business in Turkey.

It has been harder to enlist non-resident investors. These must pay for their shares in foreign exchange, thereby assuming an exchange risk. The larger the portion of the bank's funds out on loan and drawing only a fixed return, the greater is that risk. Non-resident foreign investors are therefore likely to participate only if they too are to some extent influenced by non-investment considerations. For example, they may hope to obtain profitable future business in the country and may believe that early association with the bank will put them in an advantageous position with respect to developments in the industrial field. Or they may count upon assistance from the bank or the government for their own ventures. Whatever the particular considerations influencing them, non-resident investors are likely to want assurance that they may remit any profits they may realize.[6]

[6] In PICIC (Pakistan) the non-resident foreign investors are: from the United States, the International Basic Economy Corporation (IBEC), other Rockefeller interests, the Bank of America, Transoceanic Development Corporation (Canada) and Henry J. Kaiser Company; from the United Kingdom, the Commonwealth Development Finance Company (CDFC), Imperial Chemical Industries, Associated Electrical Industries, English Electric Company and General Electric Company; and 12 Japanese foreign exchange banks.

In the ICICI (India) the non-resident foreign investors are: from the United States,

Government. An equity subscription by the government which carries full voting and dividend rights, as in the China Development Corporation or the Industrial Finance Corporation of South Africa, is in principle no different from a subscription by private investors. But the potential earning power of the private equity can be increased if the government's shares carry no dividend rights, as in the case of the Industrial Bank of Peru, or if the government accepts deferred shares which are not eligible for dividend until the privately held shares have earned a specified return.

There have been several general references, earlier in this book, to government contributions to the initial capital of several private banks. Governments gave such assistance to the Industrial Credit and Investment Corporation of India, the Pakistan Industrial Credit and Investment Corporation, the Development Finance Corporation of Ceylon and the Industrial and Mining Development Bank of Iran, in the form of non-interest-bearing 30-year advances, repayable in equal annual installments after a 15-year grace period. The Investment Credit Corporation of Austria received a government loan carrying interest at 1%, for a term of 60 years, with a 20-year grace period. The loan arrangements provide for the funds to be advanced in full at the outset of operations (except in the case of the Austrian and Iranian banks), and permit them to be invested on short term until required for financing operations.[7] These loans

---

the Bank of America, Rockefeller interests, Olin Mathieson Chemical Corporation and Westinghouse Electric International Corporation; from the United Kingdom, besides the CDFC, Associated Electrical Industries, English Electric Company, General Electric Company, Guest, Keen and Nettlefold, and Gray Dawes and Company.

In the IMDBI (Iran) non-resident foreign investors are: from the United States, Lazard Freres & Co., Chase International Investment Corporation, IBEC, and The First Boston Corporation; from the United Kingdom, Lazard Brothers & Co., Lloyds Bank, Midland Bank, English Electric Company, and Simon Carves; from France, Lazard Freres & Cie., and Banque de Paris et des Pays Bas; from Belgium, Societe Financiere de Transports et d'Entreprises Industrielles (Sofina); from Germany, Sal Oppenheim Jr. & Cie., and Deutsche Bank; from the Netherlands, Amsterdamsche Bank, Nederlandsche Handel-Maatschappij, and Hollandsche Bank-Unie; and from Italy, Banca di Credito Finanziario (Mediobanca), Societa Generale per l'Industria Mineraria e Chimica (Montecatini) and Fiat.

[7] The Government of Iran agreed to put the specified amount at the disposal of the bank "upon the bank's request and as required." The loan from the Austrian government was made one year after the bank started operations.

are from a financial standpoint quasi-equity, in that they carry no or token interest, have very long grace periods and rank after (or, in the case of the Iranian advance, *pari passu* with) the share capital in the event of liquidation.[8] For this reason the charters of the Indian and Pakistan banks provide, as noted earlier, that the advance shall be treated as equity for purposes of the prescribed debt-equity ratio. The loan agreements between the International Bank and the Iranian and Austrian institutions contain a similar provision. The charter of the Ceylon bank does not prescribe a debt-equity ratio.

Sources of Loan Capital

Domestic. Development banks, both public and private, have borrowed from the government on a conventional, fixed-interest loan basis. Some have borrowed from the public by issuing their own obligations.[9] Raising capital through bond issues has often been difficult, particularly in inflationary economies. When the Industrial Development Bank of Turkey was created, it was expected to help in promoting a capital market by selling both its shares and its obligations. But while shares have been in demand, there have been no public borrowings; the obligations would not have sold unless they paid interest at a higher rate than the bank charged its borrowers. On the other hand, the first public debenture issue of the Industrial Development Bank of Israel was fully subscribed within two hours.[10]

The Industrial Finance Corporation of India (IFCI) has had considerable success in selling its obligations, both by public issue and through negotiation with banks—a success doubtless attributable

---

[8] The governments of India, Pakistan and Ceylon reserved the right to force the banks into liquidation should the capital be impaired by as much as 30%. The government advance being junior to equity on liquidation, any losses will be met out of the advance in the first instance; the shareholders' interests will not be affected unless the total of losses should exceed the amount of the advance.

[9] Sale of the bank's obligations as a means of fostering a capital market is discussed in Chapter VIII.

[10] See page 110 for the terms of the issue. The government has provided most of the equity of the bank and holds 26% of the voting shares.

principally to the fact that its obligations carry a government guarantee. IFCI paper is eligible for rediscounting with the Reserve Bank of India, so that there is little practical difference between such obligations and government bonds. The Government Development Bank for Puerto Rico has issued securities against its own credit, and has likewise had no difficulty in selling them. Although the securities are not guaranteed by the government, the fact that the bank is government-owned has certainly been a factor in the success of the issues.

Foreign. The International Bank, the U.S. Development Loan Fund (DLF), and the U.S. International Cooperation Administration have been the principal sources of foreign loans to development banks.[11]

As noted in Chapter I, the International Bank has made loans of foreign exchange to a number of development banks. The loan proceeds are re-lent as approved by the International Bank from time to time. The Bank has authorized some of its development bank borrowers to re-lend up to a stated amount without obtaining its prior approval. For example, the Industrial Development Bank of Turkey may re-lend the proceeds of its loan without prior International Bank approval for projects requiring no more than $50,000 in foreign exchange. Under the terms of the second International Bank loan to the Industrial Credit and Investment Corporation of India, the latter may re-lend up to $100,000 for any one project without prior International Bank approval, to an aggregate of $1 million. International Bank loans, being repayable in foreign exchange, give rise to an exchange risk problem, as discussed in Chapter VI; this has in some instances caused delay in drawing on a loan.

The DLF, like the International Bank, is a source of foreign exchange loans for development banks. DLF is not required to insist upon a government guarantee, and moreover has the authority to permit repayment in local currency. Where repayment in local currency is permitted, however, the loan is denominated in dollars, thereby providing for maintenance of value; repayment must be

---

[11] See page 35 for table of International Bank and DLF loans to development banks.

made by the borrower at the rate of exchange prevailing at the time of repayment. Thus DLF loans, like International Bank loans, involve an exchange risk. As a general rule, this risk has been passed on to the ultimate borrower. DLF normally lends only for foreign exchange costs, but has on occasion agreed that a portion of the loan proceeds may be used for local currency expenditures. It has permitted development bank borrowers to re-lend as much as $250,000 to individual borrowers, without obtaining its approval. The Industrial Development Bank of Turkey, the Pakistan Industrial Credit and Investment Corporation and the Industrial and Mining Development Bank of Iran have this authority.

The ICA has made loans to development banks out of U.S.-owned local currencies received in payment for surplus agricultural commodities sold under the provisions of the Agricultural Trade Development and Assistance Act of 1954 (Public Law 480, 83rd Congress), or under provisions of the Mutual Security Act of 1954.[12] The Industrial Development Bank of Israel, the Industrial Credit and Investment Corporation of India and the Industrial Finance Corporation of India, for example, have received loans of such U.S.-owned local currencies. Such loans have generally been repayable in local currency or in dollars, at the borrower's option; until recently, the interest rate for dollar repayments was one percentage point below that applicable to repayments in local currency.

Other Sources of Funds

Agency Arrangements. Two private banks, the Industrial Development Bank of Turkey (IDB) and the Industrial and Mining

---

[12] These funds are sometimes incorrectly referred to as "counterpart" funds. Counterpart funds proper are deposits of local currencies made pursuant to the United States' requirement that foreign governments set aside in a special account the commensurate value in local currency of certain U.S. dollar aid. Such counterpart funds are the property of the local government, although they may be expended only with the approval of the United States. The government advances to the Industrial Credit and Investment Corporation of India, the Pakistan Industrial Credit and Investment Corporation and the Investment Credit Corporation of Austria, referred to earlier, were made out of counterpart funds. The Industrial Development Bank of Turkey received a counterpart credit in 1959.

Development Bank of Iran (IMDBI) have been made agents for the management of public funds, on a fee basis. The IDB administers the Marshall Plan Private Enterprise Fund for an annual fee of 3%, retained from the 7% interest charged on loans out of the Fund.[13] The Government of Iran has agreed to turn over to the IMDBI certain loan portfolios, to be managed for fifteen years. For its services, the bank will receive an annual commission of 3% of the face amount of the loans (exclusive of any loan as to which principal or interest has been in default for more than three months). Like the government advances to the Indian, Pakistan, Ceylon and Iranian banks, these agency arrangements add appreciably to earning capacity, without cost (except the cost of administration), and provide a source of immediate income. They have the important added advantage that the development bank assumes no risk of loss on the loans it makes or administers as agent.

Investment of Idle Funds. During the bank's initial period, when it is finding its way, income is likely to be low in relation to costs. It will therefore probably be necessary to consider what provision, if any, can be made to add to income through the investment of temporarily idle funds.

The purchase of securities or the making of short-term commercial loans are theoretically possible sources of income. The feasibility of the first depends on the availability of securities sufficiently marketable and safe. The second raises the question of the advisability of a development bank's entry into the field of commercial banking. In some countries there are no government securities which the bank can purchase and no corporate securities which seem liquid and safe enough for the purpose. Commercial banks may object to competition from the development bank in the field of short-term commercial lending. In any event, difficult administrative problems may be created by an attempt to combine two types of financing, calling for different kinds of portfolio management and different staff qualifications.[14]

---

[13] Before the Fund's resources were fully invested, the IDB received a flat annual fee plus a percentage of loans outstanding.

[14] The Industrial Development Bank of Turkey puts its idle funds to use by making short-term working capital loans, but regards this kind of lending as an exception to its normal policies.

International Bank Loans to Development Banks[1]

	Date of Loan Agreement	Amount (expressed in U.S. currency)	Interest Rate (including 1% commission)	Term (years)
Investment Credit Corporation of Austria	1959	9,000,000	flexible	15
Development Bank of Ethiopia[2]	1950	2,000,000	4%	20
Industrial Credit and Investment Corporation of India	1955	10,000,000	4⅜%	15
	1959	10,000,000	flexible	10 (may be extended to 14 by agreement)
Industrial and Mining Development Bank of Iran	1959	5,200,000	flexible	15
Pakistan Industrial Credit and Investment Corporation	1957	4,200,000	5¾%	15
	1959	10,000,000	flexible	10 (may be extended to 14 by agreement)
Industrial Development Bank of Turkey	1950	9,000,000	3¾%	15
	1953	9,000,000	4⅞%	15

[1] Exclusive of loans to development banks which are primarily agricultural, loans for agricultural development purposes, and loans made to a development bank as intermediary between the International Bank and pre-agreed ultimate borrowers.

[2] The government was the borrower, but the loan was made to provide foreign exchange for projects financed by the development bank, and as its proceeds were used they became part of the equity capital of the DBE.

Development Loan Fund Loans to Development Banks

	Date of Loan Agreement	Amount (in U.S. currency)	Interest Rate	Term (Years)	Currency of Repayment
Industrial and Mining Development Bank of Iran	1959	5,200,000	5¾%	15	U.S. dollars
Industrial Development Bank of Israel	1959	10,000,000	5%	10	Israeli pounds
Korean Reconstruction Bank	1959	5,000,000	5%	10	Korean hwan
Agricultural, Industrial and Real Estate Credit Bank of Lebanon	1959	5,000,000	4½%	15	U.S. dollars
Pakistan Industrial Credit and Investment Corporation	1958	4,200,000	5%	5	Pakistan rupees
	1959	10,000,000	5½%	5	Pakistan rupees
Credito Somalo	1958	2,000,000	4%	15	Italian somalos
Industrial Development Bank of Turkey	1958	10,000,000	5%	10	Turkish lira

CHAPTER IV

The Board of Directors

Boards of Public Banks

Boards of public banks capitalized entirely with public funds are often composed preponderantly, if not exclusively, of heads of ministries or departments, serving *ex officio*. Many charters provide for representation of almost every ministry or department in any way concerned with economic development matters. This has usually meant a rather large board; there are at least two public institutions with as many as 25 directors.[1] A board so constituted is likely to be slow-moving; the directors' other official duties make it difficult to schedule frequent meetings and board members often have little time to familiarize themselves with the details of investment proposals. Moreover, efficiency is likely to vary inversely with size. For these reasons, some banks have adopted the device of an executive committee authorized to take final action on the board's behalf, or to act subject to ratification by the full board. Sometimes the general manager has been given authority to act finally on certain types of proposals.[2]

Even where the charter does not prescribe representation of particular government departments, public officials are often called upon to serve as directors; sometimes members of the legislature

---

[1] Only a few banks, public or private, have more than 15 directors; most have at least five.

[2] These devices are not confined to public banks. See the discussion later in this chapter.

are appointed. This may not be in the bank's best interests. Such nominees—particularly top officials and legislators—inevitably bring with them a "political" atmosphere which may impair the effectiveness of assistance to the private sector. Moreover, they are not likely to have had much experience in industrial financing. For this reason, among others, some charters explicitly or implicitly direct the government to look elsewhere for directors; sometimes the government does so as a matter of policy.

The charter of the Corporacion de Fomento de la Produccion of Chile, for example, provides for representation of engineering, trade, manufacturers', agricultural, mining and labor associations. The charter of the Industrial Development Corporation of South Africa (IDC) provides that directors shall be chosen "for their ability and experience in business or administration, and their suitability otherwise for appointment as directors." It also declares members of the legislature to be ineligible for appointment, nomination or election to the board; moreover, no one may "remain" as director who becomes a member of parliament. While the charter thus prohibits appointment of members of the legislature, it does not expressly preclude appointment of high government officials or career civil servants. As a matter of policy, however, the IDC board has consistently been composed entirely of private citizens. In 1958 a chemical engineer (as chairman), an auditor, a farmer, an architect, a paper manufacturer and an insurance man were directors.

The charter of the Government Development Bank for Puerto Rico gives the Governor of the Commonwealth of Puerto Rico unrestricted discretion in the matter of appointment. It has been the practice to appoint private citizens as well as government officials; in the past three years, three of the seven members have been private citizens. The board of the Industrial Bank of Peru, in which the government holds 74% of the shares, is composed entirely of private citizens: industrialists, bankers, lawyers and businessmen.

Boards of Private Banks

Foreign shareholders in private banks have usually insisted on representation independently of the domestic shareholders. British investors (banks and insurance companies) in the Development Finance Corporation of Ceylon are represented by one director on the seven-member board (although the charter makes no explicit provision for representation of the foreign shareholder group). The charter of the Industrial and Mining Development Bank of Iran provides for the issuance of different classes of stock to the Iranian and the non-Iranian shareholders; the latter group will elect a majority of the board during the bank's first five years, although the interest of the group will be a minority one during that period.

Where the share capital derives from investors in several countries, each national group may want to elect its own director. This is true of the foreign shareholders in the Pakistan Industrial Credit and Investment Corporation (from the United States, Canada, the United Kingdom and Japan). Each of three national groups (the U.S. and Canadian shareholders were treated together) is entitled to appoint a director, as long as the group holds no less than a specified number of shares, or 7% of the paid-up ordinary capital, whichever is the greater. Each group is thus on an equal footing as far as board membership is concerned, although the groups from the United Kingdom and from the United States (with Canada) each subscribed 15% of the initial share capital, and the Japanese group 10%.

Governments are represented on the boards of privately controlled banks not only where they are shareholders, but also where they have given financial support in other ways. The charters of the Development Finance Corporation of Ceylon, the Industrial Credit and Investment Corporation of India and the Pakistan Industrial Credit and Investment Corporation provide for one government representative on the board; the government has the right of appointment as long as any part of its advance to the bank remains outstanding. This arrangement may be advantageous to the bank in facilitating at least preliminary government consent on projects requiring licenses, and in expediting licensing procedures. The elected initial board of the China Development Corporation includes among the sixteen members three directors and one "supervisor" who represent the government, although the charter does not specify any particular representation for the government. The government of Iran will have an "observer" on the board of the Industrial and

Mining Development Bank of Iran until its advance to the bank is repaid; the observer is entitled to all the information given to directors, but has no voting rights.[3]

The government's voice in the composition of the board of a private bank may be indirect. The largest shareholder in the Industrial Development Bank of Turkey is a bank in which the government exercises great influence; moreover, one of the seven board members is elected by the shareholders from a panel of names submitted by the Central Bank.

The government and shareholder directors do not always have the same rights, privileges and obligations, although no distinction is made as far as voting rights are concerned.[4] In the Pakistan Industrial Credit and Investment Corporation and the Development Finance Corporation of Ceylon, the government representative is ineligible to be board chairman. On the other hand, the chairman of the board of the Industrial Finance Corporation of India, who has the casting vote and is appointed by the government on the recommendation of the board, is invariably one of the government nominees.[5] Government representatives are normally not required to retire by rotation or to hold qualification shares, and those who are public officials or employees normally do not receive additional remuneration as directors.

Just as high government officials or civil servants are most frequently chosen as directors of public banks, so the industrial community commonly serves as the source of directors for a private institution. Industrial experience is unquestionably useful. But where

[3] In addition to board representation proportionate to its equity interest in the Agricultural, Industrial and Real Estate Credit Bank of Lebanon, the government appoints a delegate whose duties include ascertaining that the bank complies with the provisions of its charter and by-laws, acting as liaison between the government and the board of directors, and giving the board, upon request, his views upon loan applications. He may attend board meetings, but does not vote.

[4] The non-voting representative of the government of Iran is not actually a member of the board of the Industrial and Mining Development Bank.

[5] The government is a shareholder in the Industrial Finance Corporation of India. Moreover, for several reasons the bank stands in a special relationship to the government. Its equity is small in relation to its debt, and it has obtained most of its lendable resources by borrowing directly from the government or with the government's guarantee. The government also guarantees a minimum dividend on the privately held shares and may issue policy directives to the bank.

the country's industry is controlled by a small group, with the bank's directors drawn from this group, there is some danger that the scope of the bank's activities may be more limited than was contemplated. This possibility is the greater where all or virtually all the bank's shares are also held by the same small group or by corporate entities controlled by members of the group.

The risk may be unavoidable in an underdeveloped country, where members of this group will probably have been active sponsors of the bank and thus logical candidates for membership on the initial board. Experience nevertheless demonstrates the advantage, where feasible, of drawing on a broad segment of the private community—banking, law, commerce, insurance and even academic circles—rather than concentrating exclusively on industrial representation.[6]

In any event, it is important to the success of the bank, public or private, that its directors be men of stature in the community. Unless the board members, who set policies, are capable of inspiring confidence, private investors are neither likely to risk their funds by subscribing to the bank's capital nor to invite its participation in their business ventures.[7]

Selection of Directors

Directors of public banks and those representing the government on boards of mixed or wholly privately-owned banks are usually appointed by the country's chief executive, a Minister, the Cabinet or the legislature.[8] The private shareholder directors in a private bank established under the general corporation laws are, of course,

[6] The statute authorizing government participation in the capital of the Agricultural, Industrial and Real Estate Credit Bank of Lebanon provides that the government directors shall be qualified in agriculture, industry, finance and hotel trade and that they may not be on the government payroll.

[7] There may be some danger of going too far in this direction and selecting too high-powered a board, which will try to push the bank too fast, and which may overshadow the general manager.

[8] Government representatives on the board of the China Development Corporation were elected by the shareholders. As noted earlier, the charter does not reserve a specified number of seats for the government.

elected in accordance with the provisions of those laws. It has usually been provided that the first board shall be named by the incorporators, with the entire initial board, or some proportion of the full membership, retiring at the first general shareholders' meeting, in favor of directors elected by the shareholders. Thereafter a specified number or proportion retires annually, generally on the basis of seniority, to be succeeded by elected directors.

A variation of this procedure may be necessary where the bank is created by special statute, because there are then no private incorporators to name the first board. In the case of the Development Finance Corporation of Ceylon, it was provided that the government would appoint the first board, one director to retire each year until all appointed directors (except the government representative) were succeeded by directors elected by the shareholders. Although it may seem inconsistent with the concept of a private bank that initial directors should be appointed by the government, the difficulty is more apparent than real if (as was the case in Ceylon) the prospective private shareholders and the government agree in advance on the persons to be appointed. In this situation the initial board will represent the shareholders as fully as initial directors selected by the incorporators.

Status of the General Manager

The general manager, who is responsible for putting into effect the policies laid down by the board of directors, normally attends and participates in board meetings, so that he may present his recommendations on investment proposals. Participation in meetings has been achieved in various ways. The general manager may be a member of the board, with or without a right to vote.[9] He may merely have the right to be present at meetings and to take part in discussions. Or, without a formal right to be present at meetings, he may be invited by the board to attend.

It has sometimes been thought preferable that the general manager not have voting rights, so that he will not be required to vote, in

---

[9] Where the general manager is recruited abroad, his board membership may create a problem, by appearing to give foreign shareholder interests an unduly large representation.

his capacity as director, upon proposals he submits as chief executive officer. In other instances, it has been thought desirable to give the position the added prestige believed to attach to voting membership on the board.

The general manager of the Development Finance Corporation of Ceylon is a member of the board *ex officio,* without the right to vote. The charter of the Industrial and Mining Development Bank of Iran provides that the managing director shall have the right to attend meetings of the board and committees of the board, but without the right to vote unless he is also a director or committee member. Thus board membership does not automatically attach to the position of chief executive officer.

The general manager of the Pakistan Industrial Credit and Investment Corporation is not a member of the board, but has the right to be present at and to participate in meetings of the full board or of any committee authorized to take final action on applications. The general manager of the Industrial Development Bank of Turkey "may be invited" to participate in meetings.[10] In theory the latter formulation, in contrast to the others mentioned, places the general manager's presence at the discretion of the board. But if the manager's judgment is relied on, and if relations between the manager and the board are good, there is likely to be little practical difference among provisions which make the general manager a member of the board, permit him to participate as a matter of right or make his presence dependent upon an invitation from the board.

Conflict of Interest

Occasionally an otherwise meritorious application may be presented by an enterprise in which a board member has a financial interest, direct or indirect. Charters of public and private banks alike often anticipate such a possible conflict of interest, as much to

---

[10] In the Industrial Finance Corporation of India, where the chairman of the board is the chief executive officer, the general manager attends meetings only to assist the chairman, at the latter's discretion.

protect individual directors as to protect the bank. Here again various courses have been followed.

The charter of the Puerto Rico Industrial Development Company (PRIDCO) provides that no one may hold an executive office in PRIDCO who has a substantial direct or indirect financial interest in any privately owned business financed by, or in competition with a business engaged in or financed by, PRIDCO.

The charter of the Development Finance Corporation of Ceylon prohibits the transaction of any business with an enterprise in which one of the bank's directors is a partner, director or shareholder, or in which he has any other direct or indirect interest, except with the unanimous approval of the other directors. The charter of the Government Development Bank for Puerto Rico incorporates a similar provision. It does not, however, require unanimity, but only the consent of all directors present at a meeting "attended by at least 75% of the full board, exclusive of any interested director or directors." Directors of the Industrial Development Bank of Turkey may not enter into any "commercial" dealings with the bank directly or indirectly, on their own behalf or on behalf of others, without prior permission of the shareholders.

The charter of the Pakistan Industrial Credit and Investment Corporation illustrates still another approach: a director may contract with the bank directly or on behalf of an enterprise in which he is interested, but he must disclose the nature of his interest to the board when the arrangement is being considered, or immediately after his interest is acquired; he himself may not participate in the vote on the arrangement in question. The charter of the Industrial and Mining Development Bank of Iran provides that if a director has any personal interest, direct or indirect, in any transaction in which the bank proposes to engage, he shall disclose that fact to the board, and shall not vote on the transaction. When the board (or the central committee) of the Industrial Finance Corporation of India considers an application, any director who has any kind of interest in the applicant enterprise must withdraw from the meeting.[11]

---

[11] In certain situations a report on the loan must be sent to the government.

The appropriateness of one or another of these provisions for any given institution will depend in part upon circumstances. The private or public character of the bank may also be relevant. As has already been noted, where the industrial community is small and includes many leading citizens, the latter will probably have taken an active role in the formation of the bank and some will serve as initial directors. In these circumstances, the scope of the bank's activity would be seriously limited and its usefulness as a development instrument impaired, were it forbidden to have business relationships with any enterprise in which a director was financially interested. This is the reason why charters of some private banks require only that a director make known to his colleagues the extent and nature of his interest, provided that a substantial number of these consent to any transaction with the enterprise in question. Standards for a public institution may well be more strict, whatever the size of the industrial community, especially where the board is composed principally or wholly of public officials.

Board-Management Relationship

A development bank, like any other organization, must work out the relationship between the group which sets policy—the board of directors—and those responsible for carrying out policies once established—the management.

Experience has shown it to be essential to effective operation that the directors have full confidence in the general manager, and that they neither insist upon re-examining issues with which he has already dealt nor issue directives on details of operations. The management must, in short, have enough authority to run the bank; a really competent general manager will want to make decisions and assume responsibility for them.

At the same time, if the board of directors is not to abdicate its function, it must retain responsibility for policy decisions. Delegation of unlimited authority would be inconsistent with the directors' responsibility. Moreover, it would not be fair to the general manager, for it would expose him to all sorts of pressures which he might find it awkward or difficult to resist. It is a primary function of the board, although not usually spelled out in the charter, to give support to the general manager in his dealings with clients and to stand between him and the public. This is particularly important where the general manager is foreign.

Another aspect of the relationship between the board and management is the extent to which each participates in investment decisions. It is common, if not invariable, practice for the general manager to sift applications. Those which are outside the scope of the bank's authority, which are not consonant with its policy, etc., can be rejected out of hand. Others may be found wanting for technical or financial inadequacies of the project. Boards of directors do not normally review applications which the general manager has concluded should be rejected for reasons such as these. For the most part, they confine their deliberations to proposals which he has recommended and to applications presenting new issues of policy.

Many banks have decided that it is not feasible for the board to consider and act upon all the applications which the general manager has found meritorious. Sometimes, as noted earlier in this chapter, the size of the board makes general review of all proposals impracticable. Sometimes the directors, by reason of their full-time occupations, have little enough time for the bank's business in any case. The boards of many banks, public and private, have therefore delegated to the general manager authority to take final action on proposals in some circumstances.

The general manager of the Puerto Rico Industrial Development Company, for example, may approve proposed financing involving no more than $25,000. Proposals in excess of that figure are reviewed by the Economic Development Administrator.[12] The Industrial Development Bank of Turkey has likewise authorized its general manager to take final action on applications for loans not in excess of stated amounts, larger for short-term loans than for long-term ones. Loans for more than the specified amounts and all proposals for

[12] The Administrator, who is the head of the Economic Development Administration, a government department, serves as PRIDCO's board of directors. If the proposal before PRIDCO calls for an investment in excess of $200,000, the Administrator consults with an advisory investment committee, which includes among its members the heads of the Planning Board and of the Government Development Bank.

equity financing must be considered by the board. The President of the Government Development Bank for Puerto Rico may act on loans up to $50,000; the full board is required to concern itself only with proposals involving larger sums.

Other banks have resorted to the device of committees of the board. The Industrial Finance Corporation of India, the Pakistan Industrial Credit and Investment Corporation, the Yugoslav Investment Bank and the Corporacion de Fomento de la Produccion of Chile are among the institutions which have standing committees authorized to act in the board's behalf.

Whatever the procedure for expediting action on proposals, the board of directors is ultimately responsible for the bank's reputation and standards. Some banks have therefore made provision for periodic review by the full board of action taken in its name by the general manager or by a board committee, to assure that no decisions are made by reason of personal bias, and that there have been no inconsistencies or irregularities in dealing with applications.

PART II

Problems of Operation

CHAPTER V

Selection of Enterprises

General Considerations

Perhaps the only general observation which can be made about project selection is that there is not, and in the nature of things cannot be, any single criterion or rule. The objectives of one development bank and the policies it adopts to achieve them are likely to differ from those of other banks; moreover, those objectives and policies may vary from time to time. The types of projects that a given bank prefers to finance reflect a particular constellation of the many factors discussed below.

One basic characteristic should be mentioned at the outset. Unlike purely financial institutions for which earnings are the exclusive test of economic efficiency, development banks cannot reduce all the ingredients of investment decisions to a single measurable standard. As banks they are concerned with the financial results of investment and the consequences for their income statements and balance sheets. In this aspect of their role they apply conventional financial tests to appraise risk and expected return: the technical and financial soundness of the project, the profit history of the enterprise, the enterprise's capital structure, the value and liquidity of assets available as security, etc. But at the same time, as development organizations, they are concerned with the total impact of a project on the community, regardless of whether it is reflected in the enterprise's financial accounts.

This combination of banking and developmental criteria in investment decisions is the distinguishing mark of a development bank. All "bankable" projects are not necessarily economically important, nor is every economically important project necessarily "bankable." A development bank will not achieve its developmental objective if it devotes its limited capital exclusively to "bankable" projects, irrespective of their purpose; at the same time, as a bank—whether a public or private institution—it cannot afford regularly to ignore the financial aspects of proposals, and thereby run the risk of failing to preserve its capital intact.

The distinction between developmental and banking criteria becomes relevant where a proposed project would produce benefits for the economy, say in the form of employment opportunities or foreign exchange earnings, that would not accrue to the enterprise. If the value of these benefits could be estimated and captured for the enterprise, all projects could be ranked on a single scale of priority. But to estimate the full benefits requires valuing costs and benefits at "accounting" prices where these differ from market prices.[1] There will be differences whenever the demand and supply of a commodity, currency or service are not brought into balance by the going market price.[2]

The problems of estimating these accounting prices are formidable. It is difficult enough to estimate with any degree of assurance the expected actual costs and benefits of a project, especially where the enterprise is new, without introducing imaginary prices into calculations of the return on an investment in order to rank projects. Moreover, an estimate of the full benefits of any project would have to take account of indirect costs and benefits, often difficult to identify and virtually impossible to measure. Finally, assuming that

---

[1] See Tinbergen, *The Design of Development,* The Johns Hopkins Press, 1958, p. 36 *et seq.*

[2] For example, in a country with a chronic balance of payments problem, where loss of exchange reserves is prevented by trade and payments restrictions rather than by the exchange rate, the "accounting" cost of foreign exchange is higher than the actual cost as reflected in the official exchange rate. Where there is a labor surplus, the "accounting" cost of labor is lower than the actual or market cost as reflected in the going money wage rate.

the full benefits could be estimated, it may be impossible to capture them for the enterprise.

Economic Priority

A few banks are required, by reason of charter provisions or in the performance of special functions, to make investment decisions primarily on the basis of an enterprise's economic priority. For example, the Banco Nacional do Desenvolvimento Economico of Brazil is directed by its charter to give highest priority to railway transport, then to ports and shipping, then to electric power and next to basic industries.[3] The law authorizing government participation in the Agricultural, Industrial and Real Estate Credit Bank of Lebanon directs that the funds available to the bank shall be apportioned 2/5 to agriculture, 2/5 to industry and 1/5 to real estate projects connected with tourism. The Industrial Development Bank of Turkey may invest the Marshall Plan Private Enterprise Fund in a specified group of industries only, in an order of priority agreed between the governments of the United States and Turkey and intended to reflect the country's most urgent industrial needs. The development banks in Brazil and Chile are responsible for preparing national investment programs; this requires that they define the goals for such programs and designate the order in which projects should be undertaken for the earliest achievement of those goals.

Most banks, however, do not formally apply an economic priority test. That is, they do not establish preferred categories of industries nor do they require as a condition of financing that, for example, in a country with surplus labor, the enterprise be employment-creating, or that, in a country with balance of payments difficulties, it earn foreign exchange or replace imports.

It is true that banks have sometimes declined to finance particular kinds of undertakings, such as the manufacture of liquor or bever-

[3] The bank is authorized to alter the order of priority but has not yet done so. It has, however, shifted the emphasis of its financing from the transport and power fields, and now has a greater concern than it once did with developing a variety of growing points in the economy.

ages or the construction of race courses. But the exclusion of these enterprises is usually impelled by special reasons of policy, rather than by considerations of economic priority.[4]

The fact is that, in the less-developed countries, almost any soundly conceived productive enterprise likely to be profitable without undue tariff protection will have a sufficiently high economic priority to warrant financing by the development bank. Moreover, if the country has an effective development program, it is likely to be only in those areas designated as of relatively great economic urgency that businessmen and industrialists will be granted the official licenses and sanctions without which the project could not go forward. This is particularly true of medium- and large-scale industrial enterprises in need of imported equipment and machinery.

It may be noted here how the practice of development banks differs from that of the International Bank in this aspect of project selection. The International Bank, which lends only to governments or with a government guarantee, and which is concerned with the over-all development needs of its members, considers before granting a loan what the investment priorities of the country seeking to borrow are. If it concludes that the particular project submitted has a relatively low priority, it is in a position to suggest to the borrowing country that it would prefer to finance other projects, likely to contribute more directly and quickly to a strengthening of the economy. But a development bank created to assist the private sector is not in a position to urge alternative projects upon the industrialists and businessmen who come to it for financing. A private businessman experienced in the shipping field is not likely to be willing or able to substitute a cement plant for a shipping project because the development bank has assigned a relatively low priority to shipping ventures and declines to invest in them for that reason alone.

In the unlikely situation that two applications with comparable and satisfactory profit prospects were presented at a time when funds were insufficient to permit acceptance of both, the bank would probably consciously apply the economic priority criterion to help

[4] Indeed, in many countries where one objective of the development program is the promotion of tourism, liquor or beverage plants and race courses might have a high economic priority, and be extremely profitable as well.

it in deciding between the two. But normally banks are prepared to finance any sound productive and profitable project presented to them, provided that they have available the necessary funds, that the requisite licenses have been or can be obtained, and that the other considerations discussed in this chapter present no obstacle.

It should be noted that while a sound and profitable enterprise is normally not denied development bank assistance for economic priority considerations alone, such considerations may, on the other hand, swing the balance in favor of an enterprise whose profitability prospects are rather lower than would otherwise be deemed desirable.

Profitability

It has already been observed that all banks are concerned with the profitability of applicant enterprises, as a measure of economic efficiency. If a private enterprise is not likely to be profitable, it should normally not be encouraged to go forward. Moreover, it would be a poor investment for the bank.

This is particularly true for a private bank, which must build up reserves and earn dividends for its shareholders. It can do this only out of income on its investments and profits realized from the sale of income-producing investments out of its portfolio.

The interests of clients likewise require strict financial scrutiny of applications. Relaxed lending standards might all too readily stigmatize borrowers from the bank as unable to pass the more conventional tests applied by other financial institutions. Once prevalent, this attitude could make access to other sources of finance difficult for client enterprises.

Standards of financial scrutiny also affect the bank's ability to attract private capital both to itself and its projects. The necessary condition for such attraction, that the investing community come to have confidence in the bank's judgment, cannot develop unless strict standards of profitability are applied to proposals for financing.

At least one bank applies the profit test inversely. The Industrial Finance Corporation of India, which insists on rigorous financial tests and requires that projects be self-liquidating, tends to reject very profitable enterprises if it seems likely that these could probably obtain all the requisite finance from other sources if they really tried. It is a primary purpose of this bank to assist enterprises which cannot turn elsewhere: in the language of its charter, to make credits available to industrial concerns ". . . particularly in circumstances where normal banking accommodation is inappropriate or recourse to capital issue methods is impracticable."

The profit test is more than a conventional testing of an enterprise's economic efficiency. It has a direct bearing on the development bank's ability to perform some of its basic functions: to mobilize private investment capital for economically important projects and to develop the groundwork for a capital market. In these respects success as a development institution is directly related to success as a bank.

There are, however, banks which, while not ignoring the financial aspects of an enterprise, are prepared to subordinate considerations of return on their own investment to considerations they regard as more important. These are usually public institutions. A bank with a majority of private shareholders, which must obtain its funds from the market, is not likely to view the matter in quite the same light as a government-owned bank, which has easier access to funds.[5]

The Corporacion de Fomento de la Produccion of Chile, for example, will sometimes finance for "social" reasons. The Caisse Centrale of France sets no lower limit on the amount of individual loans, since it attaches great importance to the development of small industries in the States of the French Community. Because of the size of the enterprises concerned or for other reasons, expense of initial investigation and subsequent supervision of these investments is high and returns to the bank may not equal, or may barely cover, costs of administration. But for public banks, the social impact of an investment is a significant factor, and some are so financed that

---

[5] However, the Industrial Development Corporation of South Africa, a public bank, appears to stress profitability as much as any private bank. It is reluctant to seek repeated appropriations and looks to returns on its investments for its lendable resources.

they can absorb these "losses" or accept low returns without impairing their other functions and responsibilities.

The preceding section referred to enterprises which may produce benefits to the economy not reflected in their financial accounts. Where it appears likely that these benefits will be significant, some banks—again usually public institutions—are willing to assist such an enterprise notwithstanding the prospect of lower and later direct returns. The by-laws of the Banco Nacional do Desenvolvimento Economico of Brazil require that "the economic and financial study of the project demonstrate the feasibility and advisability of the undertaking and the assurance of repayment." However, the bank's project analysis also takes account of such matters as the extent to which the project can satisfy existing or early future demand; the effect on the balance of payments; prospects for attracting private capital; the size of the project in terms of the savings it would effect; the extent of technological improvements involved; the extent to which the enterprise would draw upon the country's natural resources and strengthen its manufacturing capacity; the enterprise's capital structure; the general effect of the enterprise upon the country's economy, including tax revenues; and the location of the project.[6] Even the Industrial Development Corporation of South Africa, which pursuant to a charter directive appraises projects as business risks, is prepared to wait longer than the normal private investor for returns on promising large projects (which may sometimes be the equivalent of accepting a reduced rate of return).

Political Considerations

Most governments respect the independence of development banks, public and private, recognizing that the bank can best fulfill its function if free to operate without interference. But if the government is determined to force the hand of a development bank, experience suggests that it is all too likely to succeed. There are ways to minimize the risk of interference. As noted in an earlier chapter,

[6] Most of these factors are, of course, relevant to the project's financial soundness, as well as to its economic priority.

fairly precise terms of reference in a charter are useful. So is a provision such as the following, from the charter of the Industrial Development Corporation of South Africa: "It shall be the duty of the corporation so to exercise its powers—(a) that every application or proposal dealt with by it is considered strictly on its economic merits, irrespective of all other considerations whatsoever . . ." Local political pressures on a private bank may perhaps be blunted if a portion of the shares is held abroad, with board representation for the foreign shareholders.

Political pressures can, of course, be exerted by private groups as well as by the government; if the bank's shares are widely held within the country, the effectiveness of pressure from dominant private groups may be reduced.

Recognizing that a willingness to finance certain types of projects may expose them to political pressures, some banks have as a matter of policy rejected all projects that may have political implications. This consideration underlies the refusal of the Industrial Development Bank of Turkey to finance hotels. Similarly, it does not finance publishing enterprises because in Turkey such enterprises are generally owned by newspapers. There are other banks which do not allow political considerations to enter into their investment decisions in any way, and which therefore attempt to evaluate economically viable projects solely on their merits. The Pakistan Industrial Credit and Investment Corporation has made two loans to finance printing presses, notwithstanding that the presses are owned by a newspaper: there is great need in Pakistan for books, especially school books and magazines. The Corporacion de Fomento de la Produccion of Chile (CORFO) and the Caisse Centrale of France, both public banks, have financed hotels. CORFO has tried to anticipate political pressure for approval of individual applications by preparing a general schedule of priorities based on the needs of various areas.

Where public pressures for particular investments have proved irresistible, some banks, like the Nacional Financiera of Mexico, insist upon a government guarantee. The Industrial Development Corporation of South Africa (IDC) once financed a project at gov-

ernment request, having concluded that the project was sound under
the prevailing political situation. But it did so only after obtaining
a government guarantee, to protect itself against a possible change
in the political situation. In the case of two other projects which the
government asked it to finance, IDC concluded that extraneous
conditions might affect the economics of the projects, and accordingly protected itself by obtaining the right to sell the investments
to the government at par.

Size of the Bank's Resources

Project preferences are considerably influenced by the size of
financial and administrative resources. Size is, of course, relative.
There may be periods in which demands do not fully engage resources. Usually, however, both the capital and personnel of development banks are limited, and projects are scrutinized accordingly.

Some banks have chosen to limit the variety of projects they will
undertake. The Industrial Development Bank of Turkey, for example, declines to finance service industries. The International
Finance Corporation received so many applications for hotel financing during its first year that it was decided to reject all such applications at least for a time. Limited resources may also place outside
limits on the riskiness of projects that a bank is prepared to consider.
For example, the Development Finance Corporation of Ceylon feels
that its funds are insufficient to permit hotel financing because of
the risks involved: even more than in other types of enterprise, the
success of a hotel depends on the quality of management and the
personality of the manager, while the opportunities for dishonesty
are particularly great. The element of risk was also a factor in the
International Finance Corporation's decision to reject applications
for hotel financing.[7]

---

[7] Some development banks which have financed hotels, such as the Caisse Centrale of France and Nacional Financiera of Mexico, have not found this to be unprofitable in the long run. The hotel financing of the Caisse has taken the form of long-term
(10-15 year) low-interest (4%) loans, rather than of equity investment.

Size of the Enterprise

Some banks, unable to assist both large and small enterprises, prefer to concentrate on the former, believing that the total economic impact of their financing will thereby be greatest. They are also influenced by the fact that the larger enterprises are usually better managed, and moreover offer a greater opportunity for training of managerial personnel. This last is an important consideration in countries where qualified managers are in short supply. But other banks believe that they can contribute most by spreading funds widely, and accordingly prefer to make a large number of loans to smaller firms.

The structure of the economy, the bank's purposes and the availability of other sources of investment funds are also relevant in formulating a preference as to the size of client enterprises. The Banco Nacional do Desenvolvimento Economico of Brazil prefers to finance large enterprises because of the importance of economies of scale for the Brazilian economy, and also because large firms find it difficult to obtain financing elsewhere. India, which has a federal constitution, has a central Industrial Finance Corporation which caters exclusively to the needs of the relatively larger industrial enterprises, those of the smaller ones being taken care of by Finance Corporations in most of the states of the federation.[8] In addition, the central government as well as each of the state governments lends directly to industrial units, particularly the medium- and small-scale ones. As a matter of principle, the Industrial Development Bank of Turkey does not finance enterprises on the crafts level, unless they have clear prospects of expanding into manufacturing concerns, or are of special importance to the economy. The Industrial Development Corporation of South Africa (IDC), however, particularly welcomes small industries. By 1958, over 60% by number, and about 14% in gross value, of all applications accepted by it were

[8] The State Finance Corporations in India have generally been operating on a minimum loan limit of the equivalent of U.S. $21,000 (Rs. 100,000) and have assisted not only public limited companies but also private limited companies, partnerships and even individuals.

from such industries. More than half the total amount of loans which the Industrial Development Bank of Israel had authorized by the end of 1958 were for sums less than the equivalent of U.S. $250,000 and over 25% were for less than the equivalent of U.S. $100,000.

The special problems and risks of small enterprise financing may restrain banks from entering this field, and the policy of normally lending only against full security may discourage smaller enterprises from applying for financing. The careful investigation and supervision which this kind of financing calls for makes it expensive. The number and variety of staff required to sift project applications and follow approved projects are likely to bear a much less direct relationship to the size of projects than to their number. The Industrial Development Corporation of South Africa has noted that in many instances the difficulties of investigating the small application are greater than those involved in applications many times as large, and that the supervision of investments in small enterprises presents unique problems with respect to management follow-up, maintenance of accurate statistical records and general organization.[9]

Many banks accordingly limit their efforts in this direction, unless they do not have to assume the administrative expense themselves. The Pakistan Industrial Credit and Investment Corporation estimates that its "break-even point" is Rs. 200,000 (U.S. $42,000) though it has on occasion lent as little as about half that amount. Rs. 500,000 (U.S. $105,000) has in the past been the normal lower limit of investments by the Industrial Credit and Investment Corporation of India.[10] The Industrial Finance Corporation of India has adopted Rs. 1 million (U.S. $210,000) as its lower limit, except for supplementary loans to existing clients and for applicants from states in which no Finance Corporation has been set up.

This does not mean that the needs of small enterprises cannot be met. Where small enterprise has appeared to be a principal vehicle for development in the private sector or where it has been public policy to develop as broad an entrepreneurial class and as great a

---

[9] IDC Annual Reports and Accounts, 1958, p. 15.
[10] The limit is to be reduced. See page 67.

diversity of small industries as possible, development banks have helped in a variety of ways. Under an "aid to small industries" program, the Government Development Bank for Puerto Rico has established a $500,000 revolving fund out of which it makes loans of not more than $10,000 for terms of no more than five years to enterprises typically capitalized at no more than $50,000. The loans may be made without security.[11] In Mexico, the Nacional Financiera administers a trust fund set up by the government for assistance to small industry. The fund rediscounts loans from private banks to small industry, and is authorized to guarantee such loans in United States dollar equivalents. As of mid-1958, the average loan rediscounted was the equivalent of $12,000;[12] the upper limit of individual loans rediscounted was the equivalent of $96,000 on loans for fixed assets and $48,000 on loans for working capital. Of the 12% per annum maximum interest charged by the private banks to borrowers, 8% is paid over to the fund as a rediscounting fee and the banks retain 4% as compensation for investigating projects and bearing the risk of loss. Nacional Financiera retains a fraction of the fund's earnings to cover administrative expenses. The Pakistan Industrial Credit and Investment Corporation, which cannot afford to make small loans directly, plans to rediscount the paper of clients of the government-sponsored Small Industries Corporation, with the latter's guarantee.

This Small Industries Corporation illustrates another, more common method of assisting small industries: creating special organizations for the purpose, sometimes as subsidiaries of the parent bank. The Caisse Centrale of France has created 14 subsidiaries located overseas to investigate and administer loans to small borrowers unable to find credit locally. The subsidiaries receive loans from the Caisse and in their turn lend to small applicants. Mention has earlier been made of the State Finance Corporations in India, which make only small investments; there are now 12. A National Small Industries Corporation works with Small Industries Service Institutes and

[11] This program was originated by the Puerto Rico Industrial Development Company, and was later adopted by the Government Development Bank.
[12] U.S. $1 = 12.49 pesos.

with an industrial extension service; still other organizations stimulate and finance cottage industries. The Pakistan Industrial Credit and Investment Corporation, together with an American firm, has sponsored a company to finance small industrialists on a participation basis.

Ownership of the Enterprise

Private or Public. Many banks, both public and private, are authorized to lend only to private enterprises. Chapter II described several of the ways in which charters define "private" enterprise, some leaving little or no room for interpretation by the board of directors, others leaving it to the board to decide whether an enterprise may be considered private.

The charter of the Ceylon bank, it will be recalled, declares an enterprise to be eligible for assistance as a "private" enterprise if no more than 20% of its capital is held by the government.

The formulation in the charter of the Pakistan Industrial Credit and Investment Corporation requires the board to decide whether, notwithstanding government financial assistance, an applicant enterprise is nevertheless "privately operated and managed" and the government's interest neither directly nor indirectly controlling.

The board of the International Finance Corporation functions under a charter directive to assist in financing "productive private enterprises in association with private investors," coupled with a provision that the fact of a public interest in an enterprise shall not necessarily preclude assistance by the Corporation. Under the first portion of this charter language, it is the Corporation's policy to exclude from consideration any undertaking which is government-owned and operated or in the management of which the government participates to any significant extent. Under the other provision, the board considers whether an enterprise which has received governmental financial assistance is nevertheless "essentially private in character." It regards a government equity interest as *prima facie* a greater obstacle to an investment on its part than government finance in the form of a loan or non-voting shares—although the size of any government loan in relation to the private equity would be material.

The charter of the Industrial Finance Corporation of Thailand provides that the existence of a government or other public interest in an enterprise shall not necessarily preclude financing by the bank if the enterprise, despite that interest, is essentially private in character. The charter further provides that no enterprise shall be considered essentially private in character if the government or any government agency holds, directly or indirectly, more than 10% of the total share capital.

The charter of the Industrial Development Bank of Turkey contains no definition of a "private" enterprise. Thus the directors may adopt whatever criteria they choose, and may consider an enterprise in which only 51% of the capital comes from private sources as "private" and hence eligible for assistance. In fact, the board interprets the term strictly, mindful of Turkey's history of statism. An enterprise in which there is any government capital is disqualified for bank assistance.

Domestic or Foreign. Of the applications which come to a development bank, those from enterprises under foreign management or control are often the best prepared and presented, simply because the staff is likely to be thoroughly familiar with the preparation of project applications and to know how to work out and put forward effectively the essentials and details of a proposal. For this reason and because the management of a foreign firm is likely to be experienced, the development bank may prefer to finance a project of a foreign firm as against an otherwise comparable project under domestic management. Sometimes, however, the feeling of the local business community and the bank's desire to help develop an entrepreneurial group within the country have led to a preference for domestic enterprises.

In this matter there appears to be some difference between the attitudes of private and of public banks: the former have normally welcomed association with foreign capital, while the latter have sometimes been reluctant to assist enterprises in which foreign capital is invested. In Brazil, for example, the government-owned Banco

Nacional do Desenvolvimento Economico as a matter of policy gives preference to local enterprises where the technical and financial qualifications of competing projects are approximately equal, or where its assistance may make the local project competitive. On the other hand, it does welcome foreign capital which brings along new technology.

In Mexico, Nacional Financiera assists enterprises in which there is foreign participation, as long as local capital holds at least a 50% interest. In new fields of production it may finance companies in which the foreign share is larger, even up to 100% foreign ownership.

Much obviously depends on the facts in each case. Even where banks normally welcome foreign companies without reservation, they may be reluctant to lend to enterprises which have ready access to foreign funds and which appear to be seeking development bank financing primarily to incur an obligation in local instead of foreign currency. There may likewise be a reluctance to lend to enterprises which can raise funds by selling shares locally but prefer to borrow in order to preserve the existing pattern of ownership and control; or a reluctance to lend to enterprises which propose to make their own contribution solely in the form of patent rights and technological assistance.

Corporate Status. Some banks decline to finance enterprises owned by individuals. They believe that the prospects for corporate enterprises, and hence for their own investment, are better than for enterprises owned or managed by individuals or partnerships, where continuity of management is not assured.[13] The Industrial Development Bank of Turkey does not flatly decline to lend to unincorporated firms, but prefers to deal with joint-stock companies; it also encourages individual applicants to incorporate. The corporate form of enterprise is not only a matter of convenience to the development bank; it paves the way for the financial participation of others at a later date, something many development banks try to encourage.[14]

[13] Special institutions have been established in India to assist individuals and private limited companies.
[14] See Chapter VIII.

Establishment or Expansion

Charters generally make no distinction between assistance to existing enterprises and to new ones. The Ceylon bank is directed "to
assist in . . . establishment, expansion and modernization." With
some variations, this is generally the declared purpose of a development bank. It is nonetheless interesting to note that of the banks
which attended the International Bank conference and which are
not subject to a charter directive to favor new or existing enterprises,
most in practice, a few as a matter of policy, emphasize the establishment of new firms.[15]

As development organizations, banks are concerned primarily to
open new fields of economic activity and to enlarge the variety of
skills of the labor force and entrepreneurial groups. Expanding the
scale or scope of existing enterprises need not have a lower economic
priority than new enterprises—the reverse may often be true—but it
has sometimes been the case that only the development bank has
been willing to supply the initiative and assume the risks involved
in new enterprise financing. The problems of expanding established
enterprises are generally less difficult. Technical and managerial
personnel and experience are already available. Furthermore, the
established enterprise often has access to sources of financing closed
to the new firm.[16]

The experience of the Industrial Development Bank of Turkey
may be cited here. At the start of operations, it financed primarily industries already well-established. Gradually, however, it has turned

[15] As of 1958, about 40% of all projects which the Industrial Credit and Investment Corporation of India had assisted were new. About two-thirds of the financing
of the Industrial Finance Corporation of India had gone to new undertakings, although
the bank's charter originally authorized loans to established enterprises only. Of the
20 projects the Pakistan Industrial Credit and Investment Corporation agreed to
finance, 10 were new industrial units. The banks in Puerto Rico, Turkey, Brazil and
Chile had likewise invested predominantly in new enterprises.

[16] It is probable that in many cases the predominance of new enterprise financing
in the bank's portfolio is less a matter of deliberate policy than a reflection of the
fact that existing enterprises have less need than new enterprises to seek development
bank assistance.

to new or less well-developed industries.[17] Other banks have followed a similar pattern. They have found that capital is not generally forthcoming for unproved ventures or for unfamiliar lines of activity, no matter how large the project's profit potential, and accordingly have concluded that they should endeavor to assist entrepreneurs to enter new fields.

A consequence of emphasizing the financing of new enterprises is that some banks have themselves become industrial promoters and planners, and have provided research services for industry. These activities are discussed in Chapter IX.

[17] At the time of the International Bank conference, some 70% of the Turkish bank's financing was going to new firms.

CHAPTER VI

Investment Terms

Size of Investment

Charters normally do not limit the size of individual investments.[1] None of the banks which participated in the International Bank conference is held to a lower limit by its charter. Only two are subject to an upper limit, and each of these limits is flexible. Except with the approval of the Ministry of Finance, the Industrial Finance Corporation of India may not lend more than a specified amount on its own authority without a government guarantee, or make more than three loans to any one borrower. The charter of the Government Development Bank for Puerto Rico provides that it may not lend to any one borrower an amount which is greater than 10% of the bank's capital and surplus; in exceptional circumstances the limit may be 25%.

However, many banks have as a matter of policy adopted financing limits. An upper limit helps to ensure a minimum acceptable diversification of investments. An announced lower limit may stave off a flood of applications for projects on which the probable returns would not meet the cost of investigation and supervision.

Actual limits vary widely. Some banks define their self-imposed limit as a proportion of their capital. The Industrial Credit and In-

[1] Regulations appended to the law which is the charter of the Agricultural, Industrial and Real Estate Credit Bank of Lebanon limit the amount of any single agricultural loan, depending on its term and whether the borrower is an individual or an agricultural or cooperative society.

vestment Corporation of India, for example, normally limits its commitment in any one undertaking to 10% of its original share capital and its government advance. Other banks will lend no more (or no less) than an absolute sum. The accompanying table illustrates for several banks the range of investments actually made; in some cases actual investments are larger or smaller than "normal policy."

Size of Investments Actually Made[1]

	Minimum	Maximum
	(U.S. $ equivalent)	
Industrial Finance Corporation of India[2]	10,500	6,300,000
Industrial Credit and Investment Corporation of India	67,410[3]	2,100,000
Pakistan Industrial Credit and Investment Corporation	21,000	2,250,000[4]
Government Development Bank for Puerto Rico	300	4,000,000
Puerto Rico Industrial Development Company	250	10,000,000
Industrial Development Corporation of South Africa	5,600	3,500,000
Development Finance Corporation of Ceylon	18,000	420,000
Banco Nacional do Desenvolvimento Economico of Brazil	11,770	23,500,000
International Finance Corporation	140,000	2,450,000

[1] As of May 1959.

[2] Single loans of less than the equivalent of $210,000 are normally made only to enterprises in States lacking a State Finance Corporation, or to supplement a loan previously made to the enterprise. Loans exceeding $2.1 million to a single enterprise or to enterprises under common management require government approval.

[3] ICICI has decided to reduce its normal lower limit from the former $105,000 equivalent to $21,000, to make possible financing of small imports of miscellaneous equipment, and loans for new projects in selected fields offering opportunity for high returns and foreign exchange savings from investments in small units of equipment.

[4] The loan for $2.25 million was exceptional; with that exception, PICIC's maximum has been $525,000.

Proportion of Capital Requirements. A policy of providing no more than a stated proportion of an enterprise's total capital requirements has the consequence of limiting the size of individual investments. Generally banks are not prepared to invest more than the owners of the enterprise are themselves willing to put up. Thus the banks normally finance no more than 50% of total capital requirements.

There are variations about this norm. For example, the Industrial Development Corporation of South Africa normally finances up to about one-third of an applicant's capital requirements, although it has on occasion financed 50%. The Banco Nacional do Desenvolvimento Economico of Brazil normally limits its participation to 60% of the cost of a private project, but may provide all the capital for a government project. The International Finance Corporation expects the private investors to put up at least half the required capital in the case of a new enterprise. For expansion of an existing enterprise it will consider providing a higher proportion of the new investment, but nevertheless requires that the total private investment in the expanded enterprise exceed the amount of its own investment. The proportion which the Government Development Bank for Puerto Rico lends depends on the assets to be financed: it finances 60% of the value of land and buildings, but only 50% of the value of equipment. The Corporacion de Fomento de la Produccion of Chile has financed from 5% to 90% of a project's total cost.

Variations in lending limits also result from the fact that "total capital requirements" are not calculated in the same way by all banks. As discussed further below, to some banks "50%" means half the capital requirements, exclusive of working capital. Other banks include working capital under appropriate circumstances. Some consider only the project being financed, whether the firm is new or established; others, like the Caisse Centrale of France, the Pakistan Industrial Credit and Investment Corporation and the Industrial Finance Corporation of India, take into account both existing and to-be-acquired assets when financing an expansion scheme, and finance up to one-half of the total.

Notwithstanding these variations, the requirement that the applicant put up substantial matching funds is general.

Financing Working Capital. Most banks distinguish between permanent and temporary working capital requirements. They generally feel that the latter should be financed at short term by commercial banks. But where the scale of operations is being permanently enlarged, permanent working capital requirements are generally considered to be as appropriate an object of long-term financing as the acquisition of fixed assets.

There are, however, differences in the readiness of banks to finance working capital and the ways in which they do so. Some banks, like the Industrial Development Corporation of South Africa (IDC), finance permanent working capital as a matter of course. Where an enterprise's operations require that substantial inventories or stocks of raw materials be on hand at all times, IDC takes these needs into account in determining total capital requirements. Nacional Financiera of Mexico finances permanent working capital where it is also lending for fixed assets, if funds for working capital are not otherwise available. The Corporacion de Fomento de la Produccion of Chile distinguishes between established and new enterprises for this purpose; it normally does not provide funds for working capital needs to the former, but may in the case of new ventures. The Industrial Finance Corporation of India (IFCI) takes account of working capital requirements only exceptionally, when an applicant can clearly demonstrate that he cannot finance them through the commercial banks on the security of goods in process, spare parts and raw materials which IFCI exempts from its mortgage charge for this purpose.[2]

Other banks, like the Banco Nacional do Desenvolvimento Economico of Brazil, the Pakistan Industrial Credit and Investment Corporation and the Caisse Centrale of France, prefer not to finance working capital needs directly. Where funds for permanent working capital cannot be raised elsewhere, these banks on occasion provide such funds indirectly, by financing a somewhat larger proportion of fixed asset capital requirements than is their normal practice.

These differences in attitude toward working capital financing reflect a variety of views. One is that permanent working capital is properly financed by the owner's equity: that the funds of the

---

[2] When IFCI's willingness to provide capital up to 50% of the total value of the assets and to exempt the stated items from its mortgage charge is made known, commercial banks are generally ready to provide the additional funds required to make up the necessary working capital. If they are not, this suggests to IFCI that perhaps the applicant should be made to raise more capital than originally contemplated from its own resources or from the money market.

entrepreneur which are released by the development bank's fixed asset financing should be used to meet permanent working capital needs. A related view is that any working capital which the enterprise itself cannot supply should properly be provided by the commercial banks. The Industrial Finance Corporation of India has found that companies which enjoy the full confidence of the commercial banks and which therefore need not ask it for working capital financing are likely to be more reliable; it has found the disciplines imposed by the commercial banks helpful in this respect. On the other hand, the Pakistan Industrial Credit and Investment Corporation, although of the opinion that permanent working capital normally should be put up by the applicant, with seasonal requirements financed by commercial bank credit, feels that enterprises can become too dependent on commercial banks; accordingly it has decided not to adopt a firm rule for its own financing.

Form of Investment

Though some charters authorize only conventional fixed-interest loans, most permit loans, equity investments or loans convertible into equity.[3] Article 5 (i) of the charter of the Development Finance Corporation of Ceylon may be taken as an illustration. It authorizes the bank to "provide finance in the form of long-term or medium-term loans with or without security, or by purchasing or subscribing for shares or other securities, or by acquiring any other interest."

Banks generally try to tailor their financing to the applicant's requirements. But other considerations are also relevant. The fact that one bank's portfolio consists predominantly of equities while another's may be almost wholly in loans reflects the combined result in a particular situation of the variety of factors discussed below.

Sources of the Bank's Funds. Banks are generally reluctant to purchase equities with borrowed funds, even where the terms of the

[3] Of the banks which participated in the International Bank conference, the Government Development Bank for Puerto Rico and the Industrial Finance Corporation of India are not authorized to make equity investments. The International Finance Corporation may not invest in capital stock or shares, but the loans it makes are not conventional fixed-interest loans; they combine certain features of both debt and equity.

loan do not preclude such use of the funds. Thus the equity portion of a bank's resources (including surplus and reserves) normally approximates the limits within which the bank may prudently make equity investments. The more conservative banks limit their equity portfolio to a fraction of this total, sometimes even to their earned surplus.[4]

Economic Environment. Under persistent inflationary conditions, the real value of debt is so quickly eroded that lending at long term without some protective provisions is tantamount to making a gift. To protect its capital, a bank operating in such an environment can be expected to emphasize equity investments. Protection of capital is not the only reason for the preference for equities. To spread the benefits of financial assistance as widely as possible and to help widen the channels through which savings can be directed to industrial investments, development banks generally try to revolve their funds as quickly as possible. In an inflation-oriented community, one of the few ways to accomplish this is by the sale of equities from portfolio. No private investor will put funds into ordinary long-term debt obligations in the face of virtually certain continued steep increases in the price level.

Various devices have been adopted to protect against inflation where financing must be provided in loan form. One is to insist upon conversion rights. The Caisse Centrale of France requires accelerated amortization of a long-term loan if the borrower's gross sales rise above a stipulated figure (the forecast of gross sales made at the time of granting the loan). The Corporacion de Fomento de la Produccion of Chile lends only with a dollar clause. Bonds carrying profit participation rights when profits pass a certain level provide similar protection.[5] So do loans with escalator clauses, tied to some specified index of prices.[6] The Industrial Development Bank of

---

[4] Chapter III notes that the long-term, interest-free government advances made to the private development banks in India, Ceylon, Pakistan, Iran and Austria may, for this purpose, also be considered as having some of the characteristics of "equity."

[5] The Industrial Development Bank of Turkey does not lend on these terms, believing that a profit-sharing provision would violate the 7% legal interest ceiling.

[6] It was the view of the banks at the International Bank conference that it was not possible fully to protect against inflation through the interest rate. See the discussion of interest policy later in this chapter.

Israel, for example, makes loans linked to the price of the dollar or to a cost-of-living index.

Preferences of the Bank. There are reasons apart from the economic environment for a preference for equity investments or loans with conversion rights. At the outset of operations, when the bank is concerned to build up reserves, meet administrative expenses, service borrowed capital and pay dividends on its share capital, the regular and immediate income generated by a loan portfolio has a greater appeal than the delayed and uncertain returns on equity investments. The Industrial Development Bank of Turkey deliberately avoided equity investment in its early years, believing it too risky for a private bank in the initial phase of operations.

But once the bank is a going concern, equity investments have many advantages. They enable the bank to share in the profitability of successful enterprises, thereby adding to the bank's income, providing a cushion against possible losses on other investments and demonstrating the attractiveness of industrial financing. By selling equity out of its portfolio, the bank can help to spread share ownership and develop a capital market.

Equity investments may have tax advantages for a bank which is not tax-exempt.[7] The Pakistan Industrial Credit and Investment Corporation, for example, is subject to a tax of 60% on its profits, but dividends on share holdings and capital gains realized from the sale of equity investments are tax-free. Similarly, in South Africa, interest payments are taxable to the recipient, but dividends on preferred shares are not.

Preferences of the Client. The form of investment is not always the bank's choice alone. The attitude of the applicant enterprise toward outside participation must be taken into account.

---

[7] The private development banks which participated in the International Bank conference are subject to income tax. The Development Finance Corporation of Ceylon pays a tax of 45%; the tax paid by the Industrial Credit and Investment Corporation of India is about the same. The income of wholly government-owned banks is usually tax-exempt. However, the Nacional Financiera of Mexico and the Industrial Finance Corporation of India, in both of which the government holds a majority interest, pay a tax of about 43% and about 51% respectively, on gross profit. The Industrial Bank for the Northern Region (Syria) of the United Arab Republic, in which the government and the Central Bank are to have only about a one-third interest, is to be tax-exempt during its first six years.

There has been considerable resistance to the surrender of share capital. Businessmen are frequently reluctant to share their ownership, because this usually means that they must disclose the details and secrets of their operations. And even if they are prepared to accept the development bank as a partner, they may be concerned that the bank's shares may be sold to rival interests or other persons they would not want as partners. The Pakistan Industrial Credit and Investment Corporation has found that some entrepreneurs would rather pay more to borrow funds elsewhere than share equity with it.

Resistance has perhaps been strongest where sizeable financing is sought from a government bank. Private firms often do not want government equity participation, fearing government interference in management.[8] Foreign firms have been particularly sensitive on this score. Even government-controlled firms may be reluctant to surrender equity. The Commonwealth Development Finance Company of the United Kingdom once considered investing in an enterprise in which a colonial government was the largest shareholder. However, the colonial government was unwilling to surrender any of its shares, preferring to reserve them for eventual sale to local interests.

Of course the situation may sometimes be otherwise: the bank may be asked to take at least a token interest as evidence that the enterprise has its blessing. This has been the experience of the Caisse Centrale of France and the Puerto Rico Industrial Development Company.

Tax consequences may affect not only the bank's but the enterprise's preference for one or another form of new financing. For example, where interest on debt is a business expense deductible from gross earnings, it may be less costly for a firm to expand by borrowing than by issuing new shares.

All these considerations are applicable to loans with conversion rights. If the bank is to supply a substantial portion of the requisite total capital, so that control as well as participation in the direction of the enterprise is involved, it may be particularly difficult to obtain conversion rights. Some banks compromise by taking conversion

---

[8] And government banks may be anxious to avoid creating the impression that funds are available only to enterprises willing to accept the government as a partner.

rights for only a portion of their loan, by accepting non-voting shares, or by giving existing shareholders a right of first refusal before they sell their shares to outsiders.[9] Where the absence of voting rights would limit the marketability of the shares, the enterprise may agree that a purchaser of the non-voting shares from the bank may exchange them for voting shares.

Finances of the Enterprise. Within the context of all these considerations, the question of the most appropriate capital structure for an enterprise is clearly of primary importance in determining the form in which a bank can best provide financing. Equity is probably the most appropriate form of financing for a new enterprise, but this is the riskiest form of investment for the bank and, until the enterprise becomes seasoned, the hardest to sell. Moreover, for the reasons already given (reluctance to accept a partner, and tax considerations), the enterprise itself may prefer to borrow. Thus loan financing may coincide with the initial preferences of both the enterprise and the bank.

But if more capital should later be needed for expansion, both the enterprise and the bank may then prefer the bank's investment to be in the form of equity. The enterprise would have a broader base on which to borrow from other sources, and the bank would be enabled to share in the growing enterprise's profits. In this situation, initial financing by way of convertible debentures has been found particularly appropriate. The Industrial Development Corporation of South Africa has normally made this kind of investment in a small or new enterprise, sometimes taking conversion rights for as much as 50% of its investment.[10]

---

[9] This does not further the objective of helping to foster a capital market, and at least one bank, the Puerto Rico Industrial Development Company, does not give first refusal rights for this reason. On the other hand, it is a standard provision of investments by the International Finance Corporation.

[10] IDC also finances established enterprises by way of convertible debenture, but then normally takes 20%-25% conversion rights. In these cases it is motivated by income and profit considerations: upon exercise of the conversion right it obtains tax-free income in the form of dividends, and shares which it may be able to sell for a tax-free capital gain. The Pakistan Industrial Credit and Investment Corporation also finances established enterprises by way of debentures, of which 25%-50% are convertible into tax-free cumulative preference shares.

The International Finance Corporation, wherever practicable, obtains share options,

Where the corporation laws do not permit authorized but unissued capital, a bank making a convertible loan must arrange in advance for the requisite increase in the enterprise's share capital when the conversion rights are exercised. Some banks obtain an assurance from the borrower that there will either be a new capital issue at that time or require one of the large shareholders to grant an option on some of his shares to the bank. Where unissued capital is permitted, banks insist that at the time the loan is made there be outstanding and remain reserved a sufficient number of unissued shares against which the conversion right may be exercised.

Once the form of an investment has been determined, the bank must make a number of related decisions about the investment contract. In the case of loans, the principal questions, to which the balance of this chapter is addressed, concern the rate of interest, the amount and type of security to be pledged and the allocation of the foreign exchange risk where the bank is lending foreign exchange. Voting rights and board representation, the principal questions relating to equity investments, are discussed elsewhere.[11]

Interest Policy[12]

Banks ordinarily try to set their loan charges to cover administrative expenses and the cost of borrowed funds, plus a margin for reserves and for profit to the share capital. For purposes of a preliminary calculation, the minimum share margin may be taken to be the minimum dividend that the bank feels it must pay to keep shareholders' funds voluntarily invested in its shares and to preserve the possibility of expanding its equity base in the future.

The cost of capital to the development bank may vary over time,

---

subscription warrants or some other form of rights to acquire shares at a predetermined price. These rights may be sold to and exercised by a private purchaser. The Corporation expects to realize capital profits through such sales, thus building up reserves and its resources for reinvestment.

[11] Voting rights are referred to briefly earlier in this chapter; board representation is discussed in Chapter VII.

[12] The specific rates cited in this section do not in all cases reflect changes which may have occurred during the latter part of 1959.

not only with changes in interest rates, but also with changes in the proportion of borrowed funds obtained from such different sources as the government (perhaps as an interest-free advance), other local lending institutions or the public, and lenders such as the International Bank or foreign governments. Nevertheless, capital costs are fairly well fixed for the bank at any moment of time.

On the other hand, there are a number of factors influencing a bank's interest policy which may be changed by decision of the bank. What items are to be included in the administrative costs to be covered out of income? If the bank is to engage in research activities and make the results available to its clients and perhaps to offer other technical assistance, on what basis are these services to be priced? Are research facilities to be made available at cost, at some nominal rate, or without charge? Should lending rates be set at a level which will encourage applicants to exhaust all other financing alternatives before approaching the bank? Does the bank, like the Industrial Development Corporation of South Africa, prefer to accumulate funds for investment out of earnings rather than by enlarging its capital, and therefore charge "the market" rate? Or does it regard itself as a source of cheap money and, like the Development Finance Corporation of Ceylon, attempt to stimulate industrial development by charging the lowest possible rates commensurate with its solvency as a bank? These are all matters of policy to be resolved before loan charges can be determined.

In practice, the basic arithmetic of lending rates has often consisted of adding two to three percentage points to the cost of money to the bank. The rate charged by the Pakistan Industrial Credit and Investment Corporation (PICIC) on rupee loans has been 6%-6½%, or 2½% above the cost to it of rupee funds. On foreign exchange loans out of the proceeds of its loan from the International Bank, PICIC's rate has been 7%-7½%, to which is added in some cases a commission based on the volume of the borrower's sales, bringing the effective rate to 8½%-10½%. Against this is the 5¾% interest PICIC pays the International Bank and the 5% interest charged on its loan from the Development Loan Fund.[13] The In-

[13] The references are to the first loans from the International Bank and DLF, respectively. The second loan from the Bank carries a flexible rate of interest, and the second DLF loan carries interest at 5½%.

dustrial Credit and Investment Corporation of India has charged 6½% on rupee loans, 7% for foreign exchange loans, as against the 4⅝% it pays on its first International Bank loan.[14] The Industrial Finance Corporation of India started off with 5%; the rate has risen to 6½%, as against 4½% paid on its borrowings. When the cost of money to the Nacional Financiera of Mexico was 5%-6%, it charged private borrowers 9%. It lends foreign exchange borrowed abroad at a 2% mark-up, and makes a similar charge when guaranteeing foreign borrowing by a client. The Development Finance Corporation of Ceylon charges 5% (6% with a 1% rebate for timely repayment), having in mind that long-term government obligations sell for 3%.

The level of lending rates cannot, of course, be fixed by independent decision of the bank. There are externally determined limits beyond which it may not be able to go. In many countries there is a legal ceiling on interest rates. The 7% rate of the Industrial Development Bank of Turkey, for example, is the legal maximum. The government of India must approve the interest rate adopted from time to time by the Industrial Finance Corporation.

A less readily identifiable but more fundamental restraint is the effect that loan charges may have on the demand for loans. That demand is not determined exclusively by the bank's interest rate. It may be stimulated by the availability of non-financial services and advice, and by the "certificate of soundness" that the bank's financing may represent in the community. Moreover, the bank may be the only source of long-term finance. On the other hand, the demand may be inhibited by the requirement that applicants disclose certain information about their enterprises, a requirement which, in the case of public banks, may make businessmen fear unwelcome investigation by tax collectors and other government officials. Tax laws may make the actual cost to the borrower somewhat different from the nominal cost of borrowing.

But with due allowance for all these considerations, there is always a level of cost beyond which a borrower will not be prepared to borrow. In some cases, the project is not expected to be sufficiently

---

[14] Its foreign exchange loan rate has subsequently risen to 7¾%, plus a ¼% fee charged once, when the loan contract is signed.

profitable to justify the loan charge. More often, a reluctance to borrow from the development bank is due simply to the fact that funds can be obtained more reasonably elsewhere—perhaps from commercial banks, or from insurance companies or equipment and materials suppliers—even if at shorter term.

A development bank does not normally wish to take business away from existing financing institutions; if it must obtain its business this way there is a reasonable presumption that no development bank is needed. This might suggest that interest rates should be set somewhat higher than the "market cost of capital," especially since the bank will be providing services and a kind of financing not available elsewhere. The market rate may be difficult to define in a country with limited financing facilities, but the going rate at which commercial banks are prepared to provide funds for varying terms under given conditions provides one convenient point of reference.

In fact, however, most of the development banks which participated in the International Bank conference charge rates somewhat lower than "the market." They try to assure that they do not compete with other sources of finance by requiring applicants to produce evidence of unsuccessful efforts to obtain financing from those sources, or by restricting their activities to types and maturities of financing which other institutions are not prepared to provide, at least to the full amounts sought.

Such rate policies are often a reflection of the fact that the development bank has been able to obtain funds more cheaply than private borrowers. Interest-free or low-cost government advances have already been mentioned; some banks may borrow with a government guarantee. The extent to which the benefits of this "cheap capital" are passed on to clients depends, of course, on whether the bank intends to be a high- or low-cost lender. It also depends on the extent to which it wishes to attract participation in its loans, to sell from its portfolio or to borrow on the collateral of its portfolio. Other investors are not likely to be interested in participating in or purchasing development bank loans at "promotional" rates below the "market rate" which they can earn elsewhere.

Banks which charge less than the "market rate" for loans must examine closely the extent to which the solvency of applicant enterprises is based on the availability of this "cheap capital." If the enterprise's prospects depend entirely on obtaining low-cost funds, there are good grounds for questioning the economic merits of the project. Moreover, it is important that the bank should not come to be regarded as an institution through which the government subsidizes uneconomic enterprises. This is an aspect of the general problem of selection of enterprises discussed in Chapter V.

Where an extremely high market rate reflects a shortage of capital, the development bank may consider it important to try to bring about a reduction in the level of interest charges by taking the lead in adopting a rate slightly below the prevailing one. Again, a private development bank which has received government financing on very favorable terms will probably not wish to invite public criticism by charging a high rate of interest for the use of its low-cost or interest-free funds.

For the banks at the International Bank conference, considerations such as these led to the adoption of rates ranging from the 5% of the Development Finance Corporation of Ceylon to the 12% charged by the Corporacion de Fomento de la Produccion of Chile. Most of the rates fall between 6% and 8%.

Some banks, such as the Industrial Credit and Investment Corporation of India, the Industrial Finance Corporation of India, the Development Finance Corporation of Ceylon, the Pakistan Industrial Credit and Investment Corporation and the Industrial Development Bank of Turkey, have adopted one rate charged uniformly to all borrowers of local currency.[15] The reason for the preference for a flat rate is generally a belief that flexible rates might expose the bank to pressures and charges of favoritism. At the same time, it may be said of a single rate that if it is set at an appropriate level for borrowers with a good credit standing, it necessarily embodies an element of subsidy for the riskier projects.

Other banks have a spread of rates, the difference between the maximum and minimum figure being commonly about one percentage point. Within this range, loan charges are fixed on the basis

[15] Borrowers from the Industrial Finance Corporation of India and the Pakistan Industrial Credit and Investment Corporation have had to agree to accept a higher rate should the bank's rate rise during the life of the loan.

of such factors as the type of enterprise, the size and term of the loan, the nature of the security and sometimes the nature of the borrower. The Nacional Financiera of Mexico, for example, charges government borrowers one percentage point less than private borrowers. The Government Development Bank for Puerto Rico gives a preferential rate (6%) to industrial borrowers, one-half percentage point below the rate on loans to hotels, tourist restaurants, supermarkets and commercial centers, and one percentage point below that for other commercial loans. The Economic Development Financing Organization in Greece charges 8%, except that hotels and tourist enterprises generally pay only 6%, and an even lower rate applies to certain types of large projects, especially during the early stage of operation. The Caisse Centrale of France charges 4½% when the loan carries conversion rights, 5½% otherwise; on 10-year loans the rate increases by ½% every year after the fifth year. For longer loans made for projects requiring heavy capital expenditure, the rate ranges from 3% to 5% without intermediate increases.

The riskiness of the enterprise is likewise a consideration. If the rate does not include a premium for unusual risks, the profit margin may be so narrow that the bank cannot build up an adequate reserve against losses. However, some banks feel that they cannot adequately compensate for the risk assumed in new ventures by charging these ventures only 1% more than established enterprises. When they wish to differentiate among borrowers as to risk, they demand conversion rights and sometimes additional security.

Loan charges tend to be highest in inflationary economies where market interest rates are also highest. The Corporacion de Fomento de la Produccion of Chile charges 12%, with the rate rising to the legal maximum (currently 16.39%) for overdue loans, against a prevailing commercial bank rate of 14%.[16] It is contemplated that the interest rate of the China Development Corporation may be 15%-16%.[17] It appears to be the general view that in most circum-

---

[16] As noted earlier, CORFO protects itself against inflation by lending with a dollar clause. Moreover, precisely because of inflationary conditions, most of its investments are in equities.

[17] At the time the development bank was established, the commercial banks charged about 20%; private lenders charged between 26% and 40%.

stances it is not possible fully to protect against inflation through the interest rate, and that it is necessary to rely upon the other devices noted earlier in this chapter.

Commitment Charge

Practice with respect to commitment charges on the undisbursed portion of a loan varies widely. The Corporacion de Fomento de la Produccion of Chile, the Banco Nacional do Desenvolvimento Economico of Brazil and the Development Finance Corporation of Ceylon make no commitment charge.[18] The Puerto Rico Industrial Development Company generally does not but has power to do so. No commitment charge is applicable to peso loans by the Nacional Financiera of Mexico, but any commitment charges paid by the bank on its foreign exchange resources are passed on to borrowers.

The Industrial Development Bank of Turkey and the International Finance Corporation charge 1%, with no exceptions.[19] The Government Development Bank for Puerto Rico charges a 1% commitment fee but waives it where the delay in drawing is caused by circumstances beyond the borrower's control; this is also the practice of the Industrial Finance Corporation of India. The Pakistan Industrial Credit and Investment Corporation charges one-fourth of 1% per three months on the highest amount standing to the credit of the loan account in that quarter.

The Commonwealth Development Finance Company of the United Kingdom has tried three techniques. On small investments it may collect a lump sum at the time the loan agreement is signed. Sometimes it charges 1% between signing and disbursement. In one case it agreed with the borrower on three disbursement dates,

---

[18] Funds of the Ceylon bank are in local currency and investments of the funds can be readily realized. Moreover, the bank has overdraft facilities with a local commercial bank.

[19] On foreign exchange loans, the Turkish bank also charges existing enterprises a commission of 1% per annum on the principal outstanding (to cover the cost of technical assistance and project study and supervision); the bank asks for founders' shares, in lieu of a commission, when lending foreign exchange to new enterprises.

and required commitment charges to be paid only if drawings should be delayed beyond those dates.

Security Policy [20]

While charters usually authorize unsecured loans, it is general practice to try to obtain the maximum security (although "character" loans for small amounts are not unknown). Even where the physical assets of an enterprise have very little resale value because, for reasons of location or design, they are not readily convertible to other purposes, a mortgage has its uses. The existence of the power of foreclosure may serve to reinforce the bank's influence over policies of an enterprise in difficulties. If that influence can be exercised sufficiently early, difficulties may be anticipated and the viability of the enterprise, the true security for the loan, may be protected.

Varying degrees of coverage are sought. The Nacional Financiera of Mexico habitually receives a mortgage on the entire industrial unit in the case of a loan for fixed assets. In the case of a loan for working capital, it has a lien on all inventories, including raw materials in process of production. The Banco Nacional do Desenvolvimento Economico of Brazil, the Industrial Credit and Investment Corporation of India, the Industrial Finance Corporation of India and the Industrial Development Bank of Turkey demand collateral valued at twice the amount of the loan.[21] The Pakistan Industrial Credit and Investment Corporation requires collateral equal to the amount of the loan. The Corporacion de Fomento de la Produccion of Chile requires collateral equal to the amount of the loan plus the aggregate of interest charges. The Development Finance Corporation of Ceylon requires collateral valued at more than the amount of the

---

[20] The policies set forth in this section, based upon information supplied by the banks concerned, in some cases reflect provisions of general local law or customary practice within the country and are not peculiar to the development bank. Moreover, while legal terms and concepts are necessarily used in the discussion of security policy and policy toward enterprises in difficulty (pp. 101 *et seq.*), the summary in the text should not be taken as an authoritative statement of the requirements of local law or as a comprehensive description of the legal techniques employed.

[21] The Industrial Credit and Investment Corporation of India also accepts bank guarantees of the full amount of the loan.

loan, the margin being determined by the type of asset pledged and the credit standing of the borrower. The Industrial Development Corporation of South Africa has no uniformly applicable requirement in this respect.

The amount of security demanded sometimes depends on the nature of the borrower. Government projects may be required to put up less security than private borrowers, and companies with widespread share ownership less than closely-held family concerns. In some countries, a good personal guarantee may be the preferred type of security, because of the difficulty of executing foreclosure judgments in the local courts. Where the borrower is a private company, particularly a family concern, the Development Finance Corporation of Ceylon and the Pakistan Industrial Credit and Investment Corporation require, in addition to other security, the personal guarantee of the directors of the enterprise for the full amount of the loan. The Industrial Development Bank of Turkey sometimes requires the personal guarantee of the shareholders in a family concern. The Industrial Development Corporation of South Africa sometimes requires that the life of the manager or proprietor of a small business be insured for its benefit, where the company's success depends essentially upon that individual. The Industrial Finance Corporation of India normally insists on the personal guarantee of two or more of the prominent directors of the concern and of the managing agency concern if there is one.

There are also differences in the types of assets acceptable as security. In view of the practical limitations of mortgages on fixed assets located outside an established industrial center, the Caisse Centrale of France in such a situation prefers some other type of security, such as personal guarantees or liens on movables. Since most banks are not normally engaged in operating enterprises, they find it important to ensure that they will acquire good title, readily saleable, if they must foreclose. In some countries this consideration leads to a refusal to accept land as security, where the land is held in the name of a clan or family or, even if held by an individual, where it may have been granted under restrictions on alienation. However, most banks accept liens on land, as well as on buildings, machinery and equipment; liens on inventories are sometimes taken.

Banks which lend for permanent working capital of course accept movable assets as security. The Pakistan Industrial Credit and Investment Corporation seeks to obtain a lien on all the firm's assets, movable and immovable, even when lending only for fixed assets. The Caisse Centrale of France sometimes requires a borrower to assign to it accounts receivable. As long as a loan from the Caisse is outstanding, the Caisse is the channel for payments to the borrower on receivables. It may withhold an appropriate amount if the borrower is delinquent in servicing the loan.

The Industrial Finance Corporation of India, in contrast, does not accept a mortgage on movables, raw materials or spare parts; only land, buildings and machinery are eligible as security. But, as is not unusual in India, it insists on a lien covering not only all existing eligible assets but all those which may be acquired while any part of its loan remains outstanding. This lien is supported by a prohibition against the creation of any new debts or liens without prior permission.[22] The bank has taken over existing debentures when it could, so that it may have a first lien.[23]

A bank cannot take a mortgage on all of an enterprise's assets and expect it to obtain financing from other sources. Where borrowers are expected to finance their working capital needs with commercial banks, there must be sufficient unencumbered assets to secure this additional financing. The Pakistan Industrial Credit and Investment Corporation (PICIC) which, as noted above, prefers to take a comprehensive mortgage initially, later releases movables to enable the borrower to obtain working capital credit from a commercial bank approved by PICIC. An alternative procedure, employed by the Development Finance Corporation of Ceylon, is for the development bank to retain a lien on all the enterprise's assets and then to give its own guarantee as security for a working capital loan from a commercial bank.

Some development banks, for example the Puerto Rico Industrial

[22] Permission to borrow is freely granted, except that the bank rarely consents where the loan is to be secured by a second mortgage on the enterprise's assets, unless the second creditor is an institution unlikely to cause difficulties for the bank.

[23] The Industrial Development Corporation of South Africa, on the other hand, does not try to take over existing mortgages because this would benefit only the former holder of the mortgage, not the borrowing enterprise.

Development Company, occasionally lend on the security of property unrelated to the business of the enterprise, such as the borrower's house. The Industrial Development Corporation of South Africa, however, feels that if it must look beyond the assets of the enterprise itself for security, the enterprise is not economic and the bank should not finance it.

The comprehensiveness of security requirements reflects, at root, the way the bank views its relationship to its client. Where a bank supplements other sources of financing and is only one among creditors, it is likely to be less encompassing in its requirements than where it is the sole or major creditor and regards itself, as does the Industrial Finance Corporation of India, as the "perpetual guardian" of its client.

Book values are generally used in valuing assets offered as security. Where the firm is new, these tend to be equal to actual costs. In the case of established firms, fixed assets are taken at their depreciated book value rather than current market value. The use of book values or historical costs is the more conservative practice in countries where, as a result of rising prices, book values understate market values and replacement costs. But where book values seem excessively low, some banks, like the Industrial Finance Corporation of India, call upon independent assessors to value the assets.

Loans in Foreign Exchange

Banks which are capitalized entirely in domestic currency are not confronted with the special problems associated with lending foreign exchange. They have only local currency to lend. Borrowers who need foreign exchange may use the proceeds of their bank loan to buy foreign exchange at the going rate from either the market or the exchange authorities; their repayment obligations to the bank remain in local currency. Neither the bank nor the borrower is affected by any change in the exchange rate.[24]

[24] Where the government has borrowed abroad to help capitalize the bank, so that some part of the bank's capital has in fact originated abroad, no exchange problem arises for the bank unless the government's foreign currency repayment obligation has been transferred to it.

But the banks which have borrowed abroad directly and have foreign exchange obligations to repay are confronted with a dilemma to which no wholly satisfactory solution has yet been found. The bank cannot prudently assume the risk of depreciation in the rate of exchange. If it did, a devaluation of any magnitude in the national currency could seriously impair its capital, especially if the devaluation occurred while the bank was new and had not yet been able to accumulate adequate reserves.[25]

The most obvious way for the bank to protect itself is by passing the risk on to the borrower, requiring that a loan in foreign exchange be repaid in foreign currency. The borrower is normally in the best position to assume the risk. Where devaluation is a consequence of inflation, the cash flow generated from operations is likely to increase sufficiently to cover increased service payments, in the absence of price controls. Moreover, it is generally agreed that as a matter of principle the risk should be borne by the borrower. If the enterprise had borrowed foreign exchange directly from abroad, it would have had to bear the risk. If the government should assume the risk, the borrower whose project had imported components would receive a subsidy. Enterprises with the largest investment in imported machines and equipment would thus receive preferential treatment and, where the exchange risk is substantial, a distorted investment pattern might be encouraged.

It is not always possible to follow this principle. The country may have no exchange controls, so that foreign exchange can be purchased against local currency in the market. Or, while there may be controls, import permits may not be difficult to obtain, and the proceeds of a local currency loan may be readily convertible into foreign exchange. In these circumstances borrowers are naturally unwilling to borrow foreign exchange directly from the development bank if they thereby assume an exchange risk—at least unless this risk is offset by a substantial differential in the interest rate.[26]

[25] The Industrial Development Bank of Turkey estimated at the International Bank conference that a 10% devaluation of the lira would mean a loss of one year's profits; a 25% devaluation would mean the loss of its accumulated profits and reserves; and a 75% devaluation would mean the loss of its share capital as well.

[26] Banks have often found themselves in competition with foreign suppliers' credits, offered at a lower rate than they can afford to charge.

If the risk is not, or cannot practicably be, passed on to the borrower, the government or the central bank has sometimes been willing to carry it. The government of Pakistan agreed to safeguard the Pakistan Industrial Credit and Investment Corporation (PICIC) against any foreign exchange loss arising out of the first International Bank loan to PICIC. The loan must be drawn down within a four-year period, and the term of the government's guarantee is similarly limited.[27] The Ethiopian government in effect bears the risk for borrowers from the Development Bank of Ethiopia.[28] In Turkey, by agreement between the government, the Central Bank and the Industrial Development Bank (IDB), the risk on the International Bank loan to IDB was assumed by the Central Bank, for a fee which IDB has passed on to its borrowers.[29]

If borrowers can obtain foreign exchange from other sources without assuming an exchange risk, and if no other provision is made for covering the risk, there is danger that the development bank's foreign exchange resources may be immobilized. This was initially the experience of the Industrial Credit and Investment Corporation of India (ICICI) on its first loan from the International Bank. ICICI refused to bear the exchange risk; borrowers would not do so as long as they could readily purchase foreign exchange from the Reserve Bank against rupees; and no provision had been made for the government to accept the risk. As a result, the International Bank loan was not drawn upon until such a severe shortage of

[27] But the guarantee continues to apply throughout the life of any transaction engaged in during that period. At the end of the period, the government and PICIC will consult on the need for continuing arrangements regarding the exchange risk. PICIC was at first required to obtain government approval of each foreign exchange loan it proposed to make; more recently, blanket approvals have been given for investment in certain types of industries.

For the second International Bank loan to PICIC, the exchange risk will not be assumed by the government; it will be passed on to borrowers from PICIC. The exchange risk under the two DLF loans is passed on to the ultimate borrower.

[28] In this case it was the government which incurred the foreign exchange obligation in the first instance. The government borrowed from the International Bank and invested the proceeds of the loan in the equity of the development bank.

[29] The Central Bank did not assume the risk on loans made by IDB prior to the date of the agreement; on these loans (17 in number) the risk is borne by the borrowers from IDB. Moreover, the exchange risk agreement does not apply to loans for imports from the United States.

foreign exchange developed that the government restricted imports to those goods for which foreign financing had been arranged. Since financing by ICICI out of its International Bank loan was considered to be within the category of foreign financing, enterprises which wished to obtain import licenses for machinery and equipment were anxious to borrow foreign exchange from ICICI even though that meant assuming the exchange risk.

Even if the government or the central bank is willing to provide insurance against the exchange risk, a difficult problem remains. Where the bank has borrowed abroad at one maturity, and has re-lent the proceeds at another and shorter maturity, repayments will accrue at a faster rate than the bank's own service obligations, and a balance will accumulate until the bank pays off its foreign debt, unless the foreign lender and the local government permit pre-payment. If this balance can be kept in foreign exchange, no foreign exchange risk will be incurred; but if under applicable exchange regulations the balance must be held in local currency and the exchange rate should depreciate, the bank will suffer a loss.

The bank can protect itself against the risk arising from different amortization schedules if the schedule of repayments on its foreign exchange debt coincides with repayment on its own loans of foreign exchange. But in most cases the bank cannot know, at the time it arranges to borrow foreign exchange, what the purpose, size and timing of its investments of these resources will be.

The International Bank is considering an arrangement for future loans to development banks designed to take care of this situation. The development bank's loan account would be credited with the requisite sums ("installments") as and when investment projects for which the bank proposes to use funds provided by the International Bank are approved by the latter. No over-all amortization schedule would be specified for the loan, except that repayment would have to be completed by an agreed date. Instead, an amortization schedule would be agreed upon for each installment at the time of crediting the installment to the loan account. Each such schedule would be based on the schedule of repayments agreed upon by the development bank and the ultimate borrower of the foreign exchange.[30] For such an arrangement to be fully effective, borrowers from the development bank should be permitted to prepay only if the bank itself may prepay to the International Bank. Alternatively, the ultimate borrower should be required to maintain the foreign exchange value of any amount prepaid, if the exchange rate should depreciate before the development bank's payment to the International Bank falls due.

Other Investment Terms

Most development bank financing contracts include a number of provisions designed to assure the most effective use of the funds provided and the maintenance of standards of financial behavior by the borrower. Some of the more usual ones are noted here; several are discussed in other chapters.

Dividend Limitations. A number of banks prohibit the payment, or limit the amount, of dividends except with their approval. The Industrial Finance Corporation of India, for example, holds its borrowers to a 6% dividend, unless it approves a higher figure.

Issue and Sale of Shares. Existing shareholders are frequently required to undertake to provide additional capital in given circumstances, and to agree that they will not dispose of their shares without the bank's approval.

Limitations on Capital Expenditures and on Borrowing. Limitations are frequently imposed on further borrowing and on the capital expenditures which may be incurred without the bank's consent. Some banks also prohibit loans or guarantees other than in the normal course of business without their consent.

Limitations on Pledges of Assets. The International Finance Corporation fortifies its unsecured loans by requiring the borrower to agree to give no mortgages or pledges of assets without equivalent security being given to the Corporation. Some banks require that their clients first obtain their consent to further liens.

---

[30] The International Bank's 1959 loan to the Investment Credit Corporation of Austria embodies these features.

Prepayment. Borrowers from the Industrial Finance Corporation of India may not prepay without the bank's consent, but no premium is charged when prepayment is permitted. Borrowers from the Caisse Centrale of France may prepay without special permission or premium, except where an option to convert is involved.[31]

Accelerated Amortization. The Government Development Bank for Puerto Rico reserves the right, in the case of loans collateralized by machinery or equipment, to require that 50% of the borrower's net profits remaining after payment of debt service be devoted to repayment of its loan. The Caisse Centrale of France, as noted earlier, applies an automatic acceleration formula to all loans for more than 10 years. After the fifth or sixth year, the Caisse requires that the amount of each installment paid by the borrower be increased by one-half (sometimes one-third) of the amount by which its gross sales exceed the gross sales forecast when the loan was made. Gross sales, rather than profit, are the measure because it is easier to determine the volume of sales.

Other Terms. It is commonly required that the borrower's properties be insured. Some banks require the borrower to refinance excessively heavy short-term indebtedness, and to consult before embarking on a new project. Banks sometimes require to be consulted on proposed managerial changes. Sometimes they place limits on compensation of directors and managers.

---

[31] The Government Development Bank for Puerto Rico imposes a premium of 5% of any amount prepaid to any first mortgage holder other than the bank. The purpose of this stipulation is to protect participants in a bank loan or purchasers of a loan from the bank.

CHAPTER VII

Relationship to Clients

Participation in Management

In contrast to development banks empowered to promote new industrial fields by establishing and operating industrial enterprises, those which are primarily financial institutions are seldom authorized to assume direct management responsibility, except to protect an investment in jeopardy. Management calls for skills so different from those employed in project or creditworthiness appraisals or in loan administration that banks which are authorized to undertake management do so infrequently and very reluctantly. Some have decided as a matter of policy not to exercise this authority at all. Even those which may manage enterprises in an emergency generally try to find other solutions.[1]

Notwithstanding unwillingness or lack of authority to participate directly in management, banks seek to keep informed of the progress and policies of their clients. They also want a convenient mechanism for offering technical and policy guidance. Some ask for a seat on the board of client enterprises as a means of accomplishing these objectives without involvement in operational responsibilities. The proposal is not always acceptable: enterprises unwilling to disclose details of their operations have been known to decline financing

---

[1] The policy of normally taking only minority participations is related to the reluctance to accept management responsibility.

conditioned on board membership. Public banks in particular have encountered this attitude, related to the disinclination of private enterprises to accept a public institution as a partner. It is not only equity investments which raise the question of policy on board representation: some banks condition their lending on the right to appoint a director. The Industrial Finance Corporation of India, for example, always insists on—although it does not always exercise—the right to appoint two directors.

In deciding whether to insist on board representation, as general policy or in a given case, banks weigh several considerations. Board membership keeps the bank informed of an enterprise's progress, but may result in involving it in the enterprise's affairs to a much greater extent than it considers desirable. The enterprise's management may be encouraged to negotiate with the bank nominee rather than directly with the bank; this is particularly likely where the nominee is a senior official of the bank. Sometimes management tends to refer every decision to the bank through its nominee. If the bank is a public institution, board representation may result in drawing the government into intra-company disputes. Some banks have therefore concluded that they can more effectively keep themselves informed, and can more satisfactorily guide and influence their clients' policies, by a device other than board membership.

The decision may be influenced by considerations other than the wish to be kept informed of developments. A public bank, for example, may conclude that private investors should be encouraged to operate without any interference from government, and may therefore normally refrain from seeking board representation.

If the bank does decide to appoint a director, it faces the problem of selecting a nominee. Designation of a staff member is perhaps the most effective way to keep informed, but this approach presents some problems. One has already been referred to, that the enterprise's management may regard the nominee as a channel for negotiation with the bank. Another is that the enterprise's board may from time to time have to make decisions on matters reviewable by the bank under the terms of the investment contract. A third difficulty, for an active bank, is that its senior officials may come to find an undue proportion of their time taken up by meetings of the boards of client enterprises.

Various approaches to these difficulties have been taken. Sometimes nominees are instructed to make plain that they do not speak for the bank and to suggest, should the management seek to negotiate through them, that the bank be approached directly. The Industrial Finance Corporation of India (IFCI) instructs its nominees not to vote on any matter which may later come before it. For example, they do not vote on proposed sales of assets, since assets normally cannot be sold by a borrower without IFCI's prior consent. The IFCI nominee may, however, join in the discussion of such matters.

Some banks, while always exacting the right to appoint a director, exercise it selectively, finding that this sufficiently eases the burden on their staff. The Industrial Finance Corporation of India exercises its right of appointment only in certain circumstances: when it has made a large loan, when the nature or some special feature of the project makes a close check desirable, or when an enterprise appears headed for difficulty. The Industrial Development Bank of Turkey appoints a director only when making equity investments and then only when it has more than a 15% interest. When appointment is put on a selective basis it is generally found desirable to make clear to the business and investment community that appointment does not necessarily indicate that the enterprise in question is risky, in difficulty or, on the contrary, extremely successful. This poses a delicate problem of public relations.

Some banks, the Industrial Finance Corporation of India, Nacional Financiera of Mexico and the Industrial Development Corporation of South Africa for example, occasionally appoint businessmen, industrialists or retired civil servants. The Puerto Rico Industrial Development Company (PRIDCO), which insists on the right to board representation only where its investment is substantial and the risks associated with the enterprise are greater than average, exercises the right rarely, and then does not select its own officials. The Caisse Centrale of France, which invests overseas, gives local persons a voice in management by drawing its nominees from the local community. Appointment of persons not associated with the bank not only helps to ease the burden on staff but avoids the difficulties of subsequent bank review of a decision in which a bank official has participated. Nevertheless the Corporacion de Fomento de la Produccion of Chile, which insists on board representation in proportion to its share of the client's equity, has on occasion designated members of its own board to represent it; so has the Development Finance Corporation of Ceylon.

It is very important that the bank be represented by men of high calibre, if the bank hopes to guide its clients' policies. Some banks take pains to impress upon their nominees that their duties and obligations vis-à-vis the enterprise are no different from those of the other directors, and that decisions should be made with the interest of the enterprise primarily in mind. The Industrial Finance Corporation of India, which does not normally seek to influence clients' policies through its nominee directors, has made it a practice, where proposed nominees are not officials of the bank, to submit their names to clients to be sure that the choice is acceptable.

As already noted, board representation is not the only way banks keep themselves informed of clients' affairs. The Pakistan Industrial Credit and Investment Corporation also receives all documents sent to board members and minutes of board meetings. Nacional Financiera of Mexico appoints an agent, usually an accountant, whose principal responsibility it is to keep Financiera informed of the client's financial status. The Caisse Centrale of France makes use of a similar device (although not in enterprises in which foreign capital has participated). The Banco Nacional do Desenvolvimento Economico of Brazil usually arranges for representation on an enterprise's auditing committee; this committee is appointed by the enterprise's shareholders and has access to its books.

Bank staff member nominees are usually required to turn over to the bank any directors' fees they may receive from the enterprise. Nominees who are not associated with the bank are generally permitted to retain directors' fees. However, the Industrial Development Corporation of South Africa (IDC) sometimes requires non-official nominees likewise to turn over any fees received, in which event IDC compensates them itself.

Provisions of Investment Contract

Investment contracts normally include provisions designed to further the common interest of the enterprise and the bank in assuring the most efficient use of the funds provided. The extent of these safeguards usually has some relation to the nature and size of the investment.

The borrower is commonly required to furnish periodic reports, technical, financial and operational. The information sought is intended to make it possible to appraise the progress of construction and the course of expenditure in relation to original work schedules and cost estimates, where funds have been made available for new facilities, and to keep generally in touch with the activities of the enterprise after those facilities are in operation. Banks try not to impose unduly burdensome reporting requirements, while at the same time assuring sufficient detail and frequency to serve their purpose. The right of periodic inspection is also normally specified.

It is usual to require enterprises to maintain adequate accounting records and to have those records checked by independent auditors. The enforcement of such provisions is often very difficult, particularly where the requirement is substantially at variance with business mores. In many of the less developed countries it is common for enterprises to keep several sets of books and to present to outsiders, including the government, information which amounts to considerably less than a full and accurate disclosure of their financial condition and operating results. Public development banks which have tried to reform these practices have met with particularly strong resistance because of their government association.[2] Nevertheless, the widespread share ownership which development banks seek to foster requires that minority shareholders be assured of reasonably complete and accurate information about the enterprise's operations. Publicly available and reliable financial information is an essential of a capital market.

[2] The Industrial Finance Corporation of India has experienced no difficulty in this matter, possibly because its loan agreements give it the right to an independent audit and inspection, at the client's expense, by an agency of the bank's choice, if and when it deems this necessary.

In some countries there are no independent public auditors; this adds to the difficulties. In Turkey, the Industrial Development Bank (IDB) had to assign its own staff to help clients inaugurate and maintain accurate financial records. Although it did not charge for the service, it met with considerable resistance at first. When auditing was made a condition of IDB financing, however, clients ceased their objections. IDB feels its insistence has materially aided in raising accounting standards in Turkey. A contribution in this field can be among the most useful achievements of a development bank.

It has of course sometimes been the case that a shortage of accounting personnel has made it difficult for the bank to meet its own needs. At least one bank, the Industrial Development Corporation of South Africa, itself trains employees with good academic qualifications and above average ability for accounts work. Sometimes it is practicable to arrange for auditing by a foreign firm.

Disbursements

It is common practice to supervise the use of loan proceeds. Disbursements are customarily made in installments, paid out at specified intervals or upon satisfactory documentary evidence of expenditures incurred for specified goods and services. The Government Development Bank for Puerto Rico disburses only after the borrower presents acceptable evidence that the equipment or machinery being financed is properly installed and operating or that the buildings being financed are constructed. During the period between approval of the loan and the installation of machinery or construction of buildings, the borrower is given a commitment letter on the strength of which interim financing can be obtained from a commercial bank. The Industrial Development Bank of Turkey sometimes pays the borrower's suppliers, rather than the borrower directly.

As noted in an earlier chapter, the borrower is generally required to provide a specified minimum proportion of the necessary funds; some banks insist that all or part of the borrower's share be put up before they will themselves disburse. The Corporation de Fomento de la Produccion of Chile, for example, usually requires that the borrower first put up at least 30% of its share. Where the Industrial Development Bank of Turkey has reason to believe that a borrower is over-committed and may not be able to put up its share, it requires the whole of the commitment to be met before it will disburse. The Caisse Centrale of France requires borrowers to begin disbursing their own funds before it disburses its own. The Industrial Finance Corporation of India requires borrowers to open a special account; it then arranges that withdrawals are so made that the stipulated proportion between the amounts to be contributed by each party is maintained.

Loan Supervision

Normally banks do not merely control the rate at which funds are withdrawn; they also scrutinize the execution and operation of the project being financed. Sometimes such supervision is broad in scope and the scrutiny very detailed. On the other hand, where the client enterprise is large and has had a long history of successful operation, there is a tendency to put supervision on a routine and minimum basis. The funds and staff at the bank's command may be limiting factors.[3]

The objective of such supervision is to keep the bank informed of progress, and to provide an opportunity for advice in anticipation of difficulties and for assistance if trouble nevertheless arises. The procedures vary from one institution to another. The reporting requirement has been referred to earlier. In the case of new enterprises, or during the initial period of a loan, reports are generally required each month; for established enterprises, or in the later stages of a loan if all is going well, semi-annual reports may suffice. It is generally thought desirable to conduct inspections once a year at a minimum, more frequently in the case of risky or new enterprises or where difficulties have arisen. However, some banks have insufficient staff to meet even a yearly inspection schedule.

[3] Arrangements for obtaining technical services and meeting the cost are discussed in Chapter X.

The internal arrangements for assigning responsibility for loan supervision vary greatly. The Industrial Development Bank of Turkey deals with the problem in two stages. The engineering department takes principal responsibility during the construction stage, visiting the project site, checking on installation of machinery, etc. The financial department is called upon only when necessary at this stage, unless the project is relatively large, in which case it participates from the start.[4] When the project begins operations, primary responsibility shifts to the financial department, which conducts two inspections a year; at this stage the engineering department participates only if necessary. A special coordinator of supervision is responsible for planning an inspection schedule for all projects; the schedule calls for a routine visit every year to all but the very smallest plants.

Supervision by the Industrial Finance Corporation of India is organized on a regional basis. Regional managers of the bank are responsible for routine inspections; if difficulties appear, the central internal audit branch conducts a special inspection. The latter also does spot-checking on the work of the regional managers. Enterprises report to the regional manager monthly for the first six months; thereafter reports may be put on a semi-annual basis. The enterprise submits balance sheets twice a year. If the expected progress is not made, the enterprise is visited by a financial inspector from the bank's staff, a technical expert borrowed from a department of government, or a private consultant.

The Caisse Centrale of France leaves inspection to its local representatives; these address themselves only to the financial aspects of the enterprise or the project.

The Industrial Development Corporation of South Africa (IDC) has adopted still another procedure. Its "after-care program" is closely linked to the initial project investigation. IDC has three investigation sections: production; financial; and commercial and economic. A group comprised of one staff member from each section is responsible for evaluating the proposal and recommending IDC action. Which of the groups supplies the coordinator depends upon the type of problem which, on the basis of initial assessment of the project,

---

[4] It is of course essential that the financial department be kept informed of any changes in the project plans which may have major financial implications.

seems likely to be the most serious. The same group is automatically responsible for subsequent supervision. The theory of this arrangement is that the members of the group which recommended the project will feel a certain responsibility toward it, and that their early and continued association with an enterprise will facilitate understanding of whatever problems may arise. The group tries to visit each enterprise as a rule once a year, more often if difficulties arise, less frequently if the enterprise is successful.

Most of the banks at the International Bank conference carry out supervisory activities at their own expense. Nacional Financiera of Mexico, however, charges clients for all supervision, even if conducted by its own staff. The loan contracts of the Industrial Finance Corporation of India (IFCI) stipulate for periodical inspection entirely at the borrower's expense, except that no portion of the salary of an IFCI official is charged to the borrower.[5] The Development Finance Corporation of Ceylon, which relies on the staff of the Ceylon Institute of Scientific and Industrial Research for supervision of its investments, requires its clients to pay the Institute's fees.

Technical Assistance

Technical assistance has proved so valuable an aid to industry that banks generally offer assistance of one kind or another, or hope to be able to do so eventually.

Many projects, particularly those sponsored by the smaller companies, require a great deal more work before they can be considered for financing. Banks are therefore often forced to consider how far they should go in helping to prepare proposals. Even with limited staff and resources, they can usually afford to do something along these lines. If the bank neither offers assistance nor arranges to have necessary services made available to prospective clients, it will very likely find itself fairly consistently rejecting applications from smaller enterprises and confining its financing to the larger companies, whose applications are usually the product of more detailed study and

[5] Private technical consultants are paid a fee; a government technical expert receives travel expenses and per diem.

greater experience. On the other hand, this specialized kind of assistance is expensive for the bank, particularly if offered before the bank can know whether it is likely to finance the project. Moreover, it calls for special skills which the bank may not have on its staff. Finally, if the bank has devoted time and expense to the preparation of a project application, it may be difficult to bring an independent, disinterested judgment to the review of the application's merits. These conflicting considerations have led some banks to do nothing in the project preparation field, some to do a little, and some to arrange for or to rely upon other institutions to assist prospective clients.

In Pakistan and Ceylon, for example, there have been established the Industrial Productivity Center and the Ceylon Institute of Scientific and Industrial Research, respectively, both public institutions.[6] The Pakistan Industrial Credit and Investment Corporation, which has authority to provide technical advice, has not done so, largely because of the expense. Meantime, it looks to the Productivity Center to assist its clients. The Development Finance Corporation of Ceylon similarly looks to the Institute. Since neither bank has yet built up an engineering or technical department, both have themselves sought advice from the institutions consulted by their clients. This is an unusual arrangement, but so far it has worked satisfactorily.

As industrialization increases, the need for development bank assistance in working out projects may decline, but there will still be need for advice of an engineering nature for projects which the bank has agreed to finance: on appropriate processes, machinery, suppliers, production methods, etc. Banks try to provide this kind of assistance to applicants in the absence of other facilities.

The Industrial Development Corporation of South Africa provides technical assistance, apart from that incident to loan supervision, only to the smaller of its clients; it encourages the larger enterprises, which can afford it, to purchase such services elsewhere. Banks often find their resources for this purpose severely strained by clients' demands. However, the Industrial Development Bank of Turkey is

---

[6] The Pakistan center is financed with United States ICA funds, while the Ceylon Institute has received assistance from the International Bank, the United Nations Technical Assistance Administration, ICA and the Colombo Plan.

in a position not only to take care of clients, without charge, but to derive income from consultant services to non-client enterprises, government agencies, commercial banks, etc., for a fee.

Technical assistance may be extended to client enterprises unrelated to the requirements of particular projects. The services provided by the Puerto Rico Industrial Development Company and its parent government department, the Economic Development Administration, include training programs for managerial and other employees; guidance through the intricacies of local government procedures; supply of industrial sites and assistance in arranging for water, electricity, transport and telephone services; plant design and construction; and leasing of "standard" and specially designed industrial buildings to investors. However, most banks, particularly private institutions, cannot afford activities on any such scale; as noted earlier, the Puerto Rican programs are conducted at government expense.

Enterprises in Difficulty

Notwithstanding careful supervision, some enterprises are bound to fall into difficulties. Nevertheless, the banks participating in the International Bank conference reported that they had had to write off only a small proportion of their total investments, generally no more than 2%, in some cases closer to 1%.

Sometimes it suffices to reschedule principal and interest payments. Sometimes the enterprise can be persuaded to engage competent technicians who can diagnose and cure the trouble. But it may become necessary for the bank to foreclose and dispose of the properties in order to save its investment.[7]

The decision whether to foreclose or to try to keep an enterprise going is of course influenced by the bank's view of the saleability of the property. Where there is reason to believe it would be difficult

[7] The Industrial Finance Corporation of India is authorized by its statutory charter to take over management or to sell the assets of an enterprise without going to court. The Nacional Financiera of Mexico also has authority to take over some enterprises without legal proceedings, under the terms of agreements with the enterprises.

to dispose of the properties (perhaps because of their location or special design), there is a disposition to make more determined efforts to rehabilitate enterprises by putting in new management, working out a financial reorganization, arranging for training of managerial personnel, assisting in devising new marketing arrangements, and so on. Where a standard kind of enterprise has failed only because of management difficulties, experience indicates that purchasers are readily attracted by the opportunity to take advantage of trained labor and the possibility of acquiring assets at a considerable saving.

Public banks, being to some degree influenced by non-investment considerations, seem more reluctant than private banks to institute foreclosure proceedings. They must take account of the political, social and general economic consequences of such action. Accordingly, where a defaulting enterprise provides needed employment opportunities, purchases semi-manufactured materials from other industries, supplies materials needed by essential industries, offers competition in what would otherwise be a monopoly situation, or for other reasons is of importance to the economy, public banks are inclined to keep the enterprise going.

The Industrial Finance Corporation of India (IFCI) follows a special procedure when it appears that a borrower may be in difficulty. This begins with a warning by mail, followed by a visit by an IFCI representative, a notice that unless specified remedial steps are taken the enterprise will be taken over and, if need be, sale of the assets. The bank is required to report periodically to the government on enterprises whose management it has taken over, and to ascertain the government's views before selling any concern to realize its investment. Reluctance to assume management responsibility more often than not leads banks to continue with the former management under their direction, pending disposition of the assets. If a purchaser is not promptly found, it has frequently been possible to lease the enterprise, sometimes with an option to purchase, until any outstanding obligation to the bank has been discharged.[8]

[8] Some charters limit the time the bank may hold on to an enterprise it has acquired even in this involuntary manner. The Government Development Bank for Puerto Rico, for example, must sell within 10 years any real estate acquired in settlement of loan obligations.

CHAPTER VIII

Methods of Fostering
a Capital Market

IN THE CHARACTERISTIC underdeveloped country, the prospects for the rapid development of a capital market are limited. The volume of private voluntary savings is relatively low to begin with, and is at any given income level not likely to be altered significantly by institutional innovations or new savings media. But the proportion of savings that may be redirected to more productive uses is in most countries quite large. The immediate objective of efforts to develop a capital market is to provide the incentives and means for the investment of savings in new ways, which will make financing more readily available for productive projects requiring more funds than entrepreneurs can readily provide. The ultimate goal is the expansion of the country's possibilities for self-sustaining economic growth.

The contribution of development banks to this end differs from country to country. The Industrial Development Corporation of South Africa (IDC), for example, was established in a country in which there were both well-developed financial institutions and savers accustomed to holding at least a portion of their savings in some form of negotiable securities. The Industrial Development Bank of Turkey (IDB) could only look forward to the capital market developments which the IDC was able to take for granted. Nevertheless, each institution has contributed to the development of capital market functions in its country, the IDC by underwriting and sales from portfolio, the IDB by sales of its own shares to the public.

Most development banks can similarly assist in the growth of a capital market. They can help directly to bridge the gap between savers and investors by selling their own obligations to the public. They can engage in portfolio sales. They can underwrite the issue of new securities. Besides pooling savings, banks can also attract direct investor participation in their own financing, thus providing still another means for channeling liquid savings to worthwhile investments. In all these ways they can contribute to gradual changes in attitudes toward direct investment in industrial securities.

But a bank cannot achieve these results unless it designs its policies accordingly. Its investment criteria must be such that investors who contemplate participating in projects, whether directly or indirectly through purchase of the bank's own securities, feel satisfied that the projects are soundly conceived and well managed and have reasonable prospects of being profitable. Perhaps the single most important way in which a development bank can lower investor resistance to committing funds to it, or to its projects, is to win public confidence in the objectivity and quality of its investments. In Puerto Rico and South Africa, investor confidence has developed to the point where the development bank's willingness to invest usually attracts private funds to the project, sometimes in a volume which makes the bank's financing in the end unnecessary. In countries with less developed financial media, and inadequate legal and institutional protection for the private investor, it may be some years before development bank approval will of itself make full private financing of projects possible. But the goal has been shown to be feasible.

Where the nucleus of a private capital market exists, development banks have been concerned to support and not impede the growth of this market in their search for profitable projects and in the formulation of operational policies. Banks are commonly required by charter to satisfy themselves, before approving an application, that financing is not available through other channels, and this is generally their policy, even in the absence of charter requirement. Applicants may be required to produce evidence of unsuccessful efforts to obtain financing elsewhere. The Industrial Finance Corporation of

India (IFCI), for example, requires an applicant to go to the market for at least part of its financing needs. However, the chances for favorable consideration are not prejudiced if good reasons are shown for an inability to obtain outside financing. IFCI is even more strict in this regard when an enterprise returns for a second loan, especially if the enterprise has been declaring a good dividend for some years.[1]

Placement of Industrial Securities

Banks can broaden investor participation in industry by selling investments from their portfolio. Each sale enlarges the supply of marketable securities and, if new buyers are attracted, enlarges the base for future sales of this kind. At the same time, bank funds are released for new investments which may one day also be added to the market supply of securities. Portfolio sales represent both the culmination and the beginning of a cycle of activities in which the bank participates, as a developer first of securities and later of markets for these securities once they have become seasoned.

Portfolio sales also provide a means for the banks gradually to dispose of enterprises which they themselves have established. Shares may be sold in small lots, the venture becoming a partnership between the bank and private investors. Further sales may be made from time to time, gradually reducing the bank's interest to a minority, and in the end the whole venture may come to be privately owned. The policy of selling gradually may also be followed with respect to shares of client enterprises. The Industrial Credit and Investment Corporation of India sells shares out of its portfolio gradually and in small quantities to avoid depressing their price, in the interests of the enterprise and other investors in it.

In this connection, it may be noted that some government banks are slow to part with their share interests. They have an understandable reluctance to dispose of successful investments and to be left

[1] Bank managers who encourage applicants first to exhaust all other financing possibilities must be sure that there is no conflict between the bank's interest policy and its desire to help develop a capital market. This point is discussed in Chapter VI, where it is noted that an interest rate below the going rate for other funds may encourage borrowers to approach the development bank first.

with those which are unable to attract the private investor.[2] Sometimes they find it difficult to obtain what they consider a fair price, sometimes they fear criticism were they to sell a bloc of shares to a particular group or individual. Particularly to meet the latter problem, and because the market is small, the Corporacion de Fomento de la Produccion of Chile, a public bank, offers shares in small lots at the current market price, generally by private sale to existing shareholders in proportion to their holdings.

Portfolio sales are only one aspect of the ordinary financing activities of the bank. But they are sufficiently important to warrant pointing each stage of the financing process to this end. The necessary condition for marketability is the established success of the enterprise and reasonable prospects for its future. The quality of the initial investment and a willingness to hold the investment until it becomes seasoned, perhaps for three or four years, is thus basic to any efforts the bank may make to sell securities from its portfolio. The form of the investment is equally important. In countries with a history of inflation, such as Turkey and Chile, equities may be the only readily marketable security. Where savers are willing to buy bonds, provided they are of fairly short maturity, some banks try to set up their loans to permit separate sale of the early maturities. Nacional Financiera of Mexico, for example, has been able to sell 5-10 year bonds but not 20-25 year bonds. In Ceylon, there are no purchasers for long-term loans, even with the development bank's guarantee.

Placement of industrial securities with the public by the underwriting of new issues has been much less common than portfolio sales in underdeveloped countries. Most development banks have had little, if any, underwriting experience. In underdeveloped countries lacking financial intermediaries with substantial resources and a fairly broad securities market, underwriting has been largely, although not exclusively, restricted to situations in which the bank has also assisted the enterprise directly.

In any event, the practice of underwriting in the less-developed countries is rather different from the practice in New York or other

---

[2] A similar difficulty, as it relates to disposition of enterprises established by the bank, is discussed in Chapter IX.

financial centers. Underwriters in Wall Street, for example, perform essentially a marketing function. They intend and expect to dispose of all the securities they underwrite and consider the operation unsuccessful if they are left with any substantial amount. But in the less-developed countries, underwriting, at least as practiced by the development banks, combines marketing and investment functions. The Industrial Credit and Investment Corporation of India (ICICI), for example, tries to attract as much private interest as possible, but does not agree to underwrite unless it is prepared and willing to keep the full amount of the issue in its portfolio.[3] ICICI will agree to underwrite even if it has no assurance, perhaps not even a reasonable expectation, that the entire issue can be placed. To the extent that private capital is attracted, ICICI feels it has performed a useful function, even though it retains in its portfolio a large part of the issue. Actually the enterprise whose securities are underwritten, as well as the private purchasers, may often prefer that the development bank retain some interest.[4]

Though the activities of underwriting and selling from portfolio place the bank in different relationships to clients, the selling problems are similar. It may be difficult to sell the securities of closely-held companies not listed on any securities exchange. The fact that the development bank has approved the securities may inspire confidence and facilitate sales. But the bank may be placed in a position in which, to preserve its own reputation, it must support these securities in the market, especially where the market is narrow. If the securities were to fall in price, the success of future sales could be severely prejudiced. A bank which enters the market to support an issue may thus find that it has acquired a majority interest in the enterprise, with all the attendant problems of management and control. Most banks accordingly are very cautious about under-

---

[3] Of 22 underwriting operations completed by May 1959 in respect to ordinary and preference shares and debentures totalling Rs. 68 million (equivalent to U.S. $14.3 million), ICICI actually took up 26% of the aggregate underwriting commitment. A very few issues required no subscription by ICICI, several required complete subscription, and most required that ICICI take up more than half.

[4] The Industrial Finance Corporation of India, which is not authorized to make equity investments, is required to dispose of any shares it acquires as a consequence of an underwriting or foreclosure, within seven years.

writing, especially where the enterprise is not well-known and established.

The Industrial Development Corporation of South Africa (IDC) once underwrote an issue which was four times over-subscribed. Unfortunately, within nine months the price of the shares had dropped by half. IDC offered to buy back at the issue price all the shares sold, with the result that it acquired a 52% interest in the enterprise, which it took over and managed. It was five years before the enterprise began to be profitable and its shares could again be sold on the market.

Another obstacle to placing industrial shares with the public has been referred to in Chapter VI. Generally, only the securities of seasoned enterprises are marketable. But when the enterprise has proved itself, the sponsors understandably want to reap the rewards of having taken the original risks. A development bank may seek to acquire shares for later public sale by conditioning its financing on an option to underwrite subsequent share issues or, in the case of a loan, by insisting on conversion rights.[5] However, if the original risk-takers insist on a right of first refusal, they may effectively prevent the bank from carrying out this plan.[6]

What can be done in this situation depends largely upon local circumstances. Company law in the Union of South Africa prohibits the grant of rights of first refusal where shares of an enterprise are both publicly-held and quoted (although the bank may agree to inform the shareholders in advance of any projected sale). Some banks, the Puerto Rico Industrial Development Company and the Nacional Financiera of Mexico, for example, decline to give first refusal rights. Others grant them occasionally. First refusal rights

---

[5] The Industrial Development Corporation of South Africa has on occasion obtained an option to take up shares against unpaid installments of loan principal or for cash.

[6] The reluctance of enterprises to permit public offerings of their shares may be overcome by statutory incentives, which the development bank may advocate even though it cannot itself offer them. For example, Puerto Rico is considering extending the period of tax exemption for enterprises which sell a certain proportion of their shares to the local investing public, and giving special inheritance tax treatment to estates which hold local corporate industrial issues.

are generally a matter for negotiation with the client.[7] Sometimes, although the right has been given, banks have been able to persuade existing shareholders not to exercise it.

Sales of Industrial Securities with the Bank's Guarantee

The advantages of placing industrial securities directly with the public are clear. Developing a willingness to hold securities is an ultimate goal of efforts to develop a capital market. This may be accelerated through the sale of clients' securities with the bank's guarantee. The investor thereby obtains the additional protection of a direct claim upon the bank's resources in case of trouble. From the standpoint of the institutional investor, a security of this kind would have a great attraction. But it may seem less desirable from the standpoint of the bank, since widespread portfolio sales with the bank's guarantee might well narrow the market for its own obligations.

Sale of the Bank's Own Obligations

Some banks have issued their own obligations to the public. This avoids many of the difficulties inherent in selling industrial securities directly. The investor need not appraise the merits of particular enterprises. He need decide only whether he has sufficient confidence in the management of the bank and in its investment decisions to commit to it any part of his savings. Some banks have arranged for redemption of their obligations at face value and for a minimum guaranteed return, thereby adding to the appeal of the obligations by endowing them with liquidity, safety and an attractive yield. It should, however, be noted that sale of the bank's own obligations

[7] The International Finance Corporation has almost invariably given the sponsors or the enterprise itself a right of first refusal as to all or a part of its interest. It always gives its partners an assurance that it will not sell to parties to whom its partners can properly object.

does not necessarily broaden the market for industrial securities, particularly where the obligations carry special guarantee and redemption privileges. This is essentially a device for enlarging the bank's resources, i.e., for channeling funds through the bank to industry. The bank itself is the capital market instrument.

Only a few of the banks which participated in the International Bank conference had, by then, issued their own obligations.[8] These included the Industrial Development Corporation of South Africa and the Industrial Finance Corporation of India, whose bonds carried a government guarantee. The Industrial Development Bank of Israel has had two successful issues of 6% debentures and has plans for a third, to carry a participation in profits as well as fixed interest. The debentures already issued are secured by a floating charge on the assets of the bank, and are linked to the price of the dollar, with an option (exercisable within a fixed period) to convert this linking to a link to the cost-of-living index.

The Industrial Development Corporation of South Africa once sold its obligations to raise funds for a specific project, rather than to add to the total of its general investment resources. This device might be useful in other countries as a means of attracting the savings of the probable beneficiaries of a given project, who are likely to have a special interest in its success. It could at the same time have the important incidental effect of helping to develop investor interests and attitudes that may later be receptive to other securities sold directly from the bank's portfolio.

A practice of the Nacional Financiera of Mexico is also of interest. About 1940 Financiera began to offer participation certificates to the public issued against a fund of shares and bonds held by Financiera. At first these represented a form of time deposit redeemable nominally on 90 days' notice, in practice at sight. They did not carry any property rights to the securities backing them. The certificates now represent co-ownership of a designated block of securities in Financiera's portfolio, composed half of industrial equities and half of fixed-yield obligations. Thus the certificates provide a variable

---

[8] Only one, the Corporacion de Fomento de la Produccion of Chile, lacked authority to do so.

return. Five years after issue, the certificates are callable in the underlying securities or in cash at par. By putting both blue chip and new shares into each package, Financiera has tried to establish a market for new securities. It is Financiera's policy, when asked to lend to a family enterprise, to try to persuade the enterprise to accept equity participation instead; the device of the certificates is used to broaden the owership base.

The cases cited suggest that in many countries the issue of development bank obligations tailored to local situations might well make an important contribution to the growth of a capital market.

Participations

Since the average investor is not in a position to appraise the technical, financial and managerial aspects of an enterprise or project, often the best way to encourage him to invest in industry is to provide him with an opportunity to participate in such an investment together with a development bank.[9] This presupposes, of course, that investors have confidence in the bank's judgment. It is an equally necessary condition that the bank have established a wide network of contact with potential investors. To this end, some banks have sought to keep potential investors within the country regularly informed of their activities and of new investment opportunities.

Participation by foreign investors has not been very widespread. In Turkey the balance of payments situation has hampered the efforts of the Industrial Development Bank in this field. Other banks have been able to accomplish somewhat more. The Corporacion de Fomento de la Produccion of Chile has established a special committee to invite foreign participation in attractive projects, and has made contacts through its New York office and in Europe. At the time of the International Bank conference, about $150 million in foreign participations had been approved. The Industrial Development Corporation of South Africa has attracted a substantial

[9] Private institutional capital often participates in International Bank loans in this way.

degree of participation by foreign enterprises.[10] But development banks in general are not well equipped to discover potential participants or to take the initiative in developing leads. This was one consideration which led to the establishment of the International Finance Corporation. Development banks have, however, encouraged foreign investment in other ways: directly, by selling their own obligations abroad, and by giving information and advice to existing and potential foreign investors; and indirectly, by sponsoring favorable exchange and fiscal regulations.

Development banks may likewise participate in financing by other banking institutions. But of the banks which took part in the International Bank conference, only the Government Development Bank for Puerto Rico (GDB) and the Industrial Development Corporation of South Africa had done so. The GDB has established an advisory committee of prominent local bankers and businessmen for the purpose, among others, of assisting in coordinating its lending activities with those of the commercial banks. It expects this to lead to an increase in the number of its participations with the commercial banks, which have been interested in purchasing short-term portions of GDB's portfolio.

An active capital market will not, of course, follow automatically upon establishment of a development bank. The real question is whether the bank can do anything to make a beginning. The experience recounted at the International Bank conference suggests that banks not only can take, but have taken, significant first steps in this direction.

The International Bank's own experience with finding local capital for industrial projects has convinced it of both the importance and potentialities of activity in this field. For example, the government of Pakistan sought an International Bank loan for a paper mill for which the government had supplied all the equity. The Bank, being reluctant to lend because of the plant's governmental ownership, first persuaded the government to offer shares to the

---

[10] The Government Development Bank for Puerto Rico has made large investments in Puerto Rican industry in participation with institutional investors from the mainland United States, and assists in attracting private external financing through its contacts with financial institutions and investors in the United States.

public, with the result that 70% of the equity is now in private hands. Again at the International Bank's urging, shares in a natural gas transmission company in Pakistan were offered publicly; three-quarters of the equity is now held by private investors in Pakistan and the United Kingdom. In both instances local "informed" sources had predicted that the issues would not be fully taken up and in both the issues were oversubscribed, many small investors being among the purchasers. A public offering of shares in a textile plant in Ethiopia was likewise a success, notwithstanding a general belief that there was little private capital available for industrial investment. The response of small investors to the second issue of shares in the Turkish development bank has already been mentioned.[11]

[11] Other instances of a growing receptivity on the part of small savers to industrial investment could be cited. For example, it has been reported that the first share issue by a public company in Nigeria, in the spring of 1959, was substantially oversubscribed, with almost 1,200 of total applications being for only 10 shares, the minimum number for which application could be made.

CHAPTER IX

Entrepreneurial and Informational Activity

DEVELOPMENT BANKS, both public and private, have engaged in a variety of non-financial activities which may be described as entrepreneurial. They have undertaken research and surveys to uncover new investment opportunities. They have tried, both by making investment opportunities widely known and by direct solicitation, to persuade private industrialists to take up these or other new lines of endeavor. They have established enterprises themselves if efforts to interest private capital have proved unsuccessful. And they have informed the public—businessmen, industrialists, investors—of the type and extent of the services they are equipped to provide.

Research and Surveys

The public banks have done most work in the research and survey fields. Such activities are expensive if carried out on more than a very limited scale, and may not produce an immediate return. Public banks can more readily afford the cost and need not be concerned to justify such non-revenue-producing expenditures to shareholders. Moreover, since research and surveys may prove beneficial to the economy as a whole, they are more easily justified by a public institution.

Investigations are generally directed to areas in which the country enjoys some natural advantage; to products for which the market is being met wholly or largely by imports or which have export possibilities; and to industries which are labor-intensive or which draw heavily on locally produced raw materials. The Corporacion de Fomento de la Produccion of Chile (CORFO) does research to find practicable projects in poorly developed sectors such as agriculture, and in the natural resource field; it has also undertaken a geological survey. Because of the way CORFO is financed, the fact that this work is non-revenue-producing presents no problem. Funds appropriated to CORFO are earmarked for development or for investment. Development funds may be expended without expectation of return, and it is with these that CORFO finances research and surveys.

Public banks may make some charge for permitting private industrialists or investors to use their studies, but generally are prepared to supply the material irrespective of whether the entrepreneur intends to return to them for financing.

Where other government agencies are engaged in survey or research work, public banks are not likely to undertake it. In France, for example, government agencies conduct research on mining, rubber, oil and cotton in the states of the French community, and the Caisse Centrale has accordingly confined its assistance to financing. Nacional Financiera of Mexico has a small technical research staff and sometimes engages technicians for special studies, but mainly relies on the industrial research department of the Bank of Mexico.

The extent of research and survey work which private development banks do is as a rule directly related to the extent to which they are able to pass the cost on to their clients. The Industrial Development Bank of Turkey, for example, confines its investigations to areas reasonably likely to be attractive to private investors or which it is prepared to enter itself. At the same time, it has built up a strong technical staff and undertakes special studies on order and for a fee, for clients and non-clients alike. In some countries, Ceylon and Pakistan for example, there has been no immediate need for the private development banks to carry out industrial research and surveys, because public agencies engage in these activities.

Promotional Work

Many banks systematically try to interest private investors in particular investment opportunities. Some address themselves only to local investors; others try to reach foreign capital as well. Often the very fact that the development bank has shown interest in a particular field has drawn a response from private capital. For example, after the Industrial Development Corporation of South Africa investigated the possibilities of productive use of non-ferrous metal scrap, three private projects making use of the scrap were started.

The economic environment may call for considerable promotional effort by the bank. This was the case when the Development Bank of Ethiopia (DBE) was created. The business community showed little entrepreneurial spirit and legislative measures designed to encourage and protect private investment were inadequate. The bank could of course do little about the legislative inadequacies. However, there was clearly an opportunity for it to mark out fields attractive to private capital, to publicize the results of its study, and to plan industrial and commercial agriculture projects to offset the lack of entrepreneurship on the private side.

At the outset of operations the DBE issued a statement of loan policy which declared in part:

> "The bank has some responsibilities of leadership. It should not wait in every case until someone else evolves a plan for increasing industrial and agricultural production and comes to the bank for a loan. The bank itself should study ways and means of increasing production in industry and agriculture and take steps to interest borrowers therein, even to the extent of assisting in the organization of companies or cooperatives and planning their projects. The bank must be aggressive in lending its money for the purposes stated in the charter."

Unfortunately the bank could not find staff experienced in promotional work and, notwithstanding its declaration of policy, was able to do little in practice to stimulate new projects or explore new opportunities for industrial investment. Its financing was directed principally to the expansion of existing production or the improvement of existing facilities. Eventually its lending reached a plateau, for want not of funds but of entrepreneurs.

The International Bank, which helped to establish the DBE, then worked out an arrangement with the Herstelbank (the Reconstruction Bank) in the Netherlands, under which the latter has helped to supply the DBE with industrial and agricultural staff experienced in promotional work. The United Nations Technical Assistance Administration met the cost of the salaries of these technicians for the first year. This strengthening of technical staff has led to a more intensive effort to seek out opportunities for financing. As a result, the bank has had more industrial projects under active consideration than ever before and for the first time has been able to investigate the possibilities for investment in relatively large-scale agriculture.

Establishment and Operation of Enterprises

Often a bank unsuccessful in its efforts to persuade private industrialists to go into a venture has gone ahead with the project itself, hoping that the project would be taken over by private capital, once it was shown to be profitable.

Several public banks have achieved some notable successes in this activity. For example, the Industrial Development Corporation of South Africa (IDC) concluded after investigation that worsted manufacture, making use of South African wool, could be a profitable undertaking. Having tried and failed to interest South African wool producers and overseas industrialists in starting such an industry, IDC obtained permission from the Governor-General to set up an enterprise itself. The plant proved highly profitable, and private capital was encouraged to invest in the industry. Ultimately eight textile mills came into operation; in only one of these did IDC hold a majority interest.

Similarly, public funds were put into hotels in Puerto Rico because, while there was need for new facilities, private capital displayed no interest in creating them. Public funds constituted 92% of the capital invested in the first large new hotel; in the next, only 67% of the capital came from the public development banks; in the next two, all but 8% of the total investment came from private sources.

A private bank is much less likely to set up an enterprise itself. It is under greater pressure to keep its capital intact and consequently more reluctant to risk any substantial part of it in an unfamiliar line of activity. Private banks prefer to open fields of activity to private investors by contributing to the capital requirements of a new enterprise, providing technical assistance, or following some other course short of taking the full risk and responsibility themselves.

As a general rule, development banks have not themselves tried to run enterprises which they have established, but have called in private companies to take over management responsibility entirely or to share it. Industrial management calls for skills which most banks lack. The early experience of the Puerto Rico Industrial Development Company (PRIDCO), one of the few banks which has endeavored to operate commercial enterprises itself, illustrates the difficulties. During World War II, competent management for new enterprises was everywhere in even shorter supply than is normally the case, and PRIDCO found that those who were qualified to assume managerial responsibility were reluctant to associate themselves with publicly-owned manufacturing enterprises. Government civil servants were accordingly placed in top management positions for the five commercial enterprises PRIDCO then owned. These officials found their time taken up with day-to-day problems. They had little if any knowledge of sales promotion and the techniques of product distribution. Moreover, negotiations with labor were complicated by the governmental status of management. Principally as a consequence of these difficulties, only one of the enterprises proved profitable.

Development banks have often been reluctant to dispose of their enterprises. Where the enterprise has been started primarily in the hope of attracting private capital, banks are prepared in principle to sell when they receive a satisfactory offer. But since investors are generally interested in only the most profitable enterprises, the bank risks being left with the marginal or loss undertakings, a prospect pleasing to neither a private nor a public institution. The problem is particularly acute for the latter, which may be confronted with political pressures both to retain profitable enterprises and to continue to operate those which, though unprofitable, provide needed employment. Nevertheless, the Puerto Rico Industrial Development Company sold all five of the industrial enterprises referred to above. It continues to hold two hotels, leased for operation to private companies. Three of the four concerns started by the Industrial Development Corporation of South Africa were sold outright or in part to private interests.

Information Programs

By and large, the information programs of public banks, like their research and survey programs, are more extensive than those of the private institutions, probably because the former have been better able to meet the cost. Sometimes the government has assumed the expense directly, where the bank has an important role in a public development program.

The information program of the Government Development Bank for Puerto Rico (GDB) has several aspects. Enterprises which the GDB has financed display conspicuous red, white and blue legends stating that the bank has assisted them. The bank publishes a quarterly report to investors in Puerto Rican securities, which covers financial events and significant political, economic and social developments in Puerto Rico, and is distributed widely within the mainland United States and Puerto Rico.[1]

[1] As an aspect of its functions as fiscal agent for the Commonwealth of Puerto Rico, the municipalities and the public corporations, the bank also conducts a promotional program aimed at broadening the market for Puerto Rican public securities. This includes directing a steady flow of information to United States financial publications, arranging for groups of financial editors, commercial and investment bankers and institutional investors to come to Puerto Rico, and maintaining a New York office, which both facilitates the spread of information about Puerto Rico and helps to keep the bank informed of conditions in the U.S. money market. The cost of this credit information program was formerly met by the bank, but since 1958 appropriated funds have been made available for it.

The non-financial services of the Puerto Rico Industrial Development Company (PRIDCO) (provision of industrial sites, construction of plants to specifications, leasing of industrial buildings, training of employees, etc.) are extensively publicized, although not by PRIDCO itself. Under the public development plan of Puerto Rico, the Economic Development Administration (EDA), the government department to which PRIDCO is related through its board of directors, conducts a promotional program to encourage the growth of manufacturing industry in Puerto Rico. This program describes in detail the facilities PRIDCO is equipped to provide. EDA arranges for press, periodical and direct mail advertising, and radio and television programs; it sends periodic reports to selected industrialists, commercial and investment bankers and institutional investors.

The private banks have not had the resources to undertake programs of comparable scope. The respective governments have assisted these banks financially, but have not systematically publicized their facilities. The Industrial Development Bank of Turkey undertook to do this in its own behalf in its first years, sending its officials on extensive tours throughout the country; this program proved highly successful in producing applications for financing.

CHAPTER X

Procedures and Staff

Procedures

It is common practice to require applicants for financing, as a first step, to answer a questionnaire designed to provide information about the applicant and the proposed project. The Industrial Development Bank of Turkey makes the replies to its very detailed questionnaire the basis of an initial project report. The questionnaire employed by the two Puerto Rican institutions is sufficiently broad in scope to serve the purposes of two other government agencies which assist private industry.[1]

Some banks merely indicate the general nature of the data to be submitted, leaving the applicant to decide how much detail to supply and in what form. The Pakistan Industrial Credit and Investment Corporation, the Industrial Credit and Investment Corporation of India, the Corporacion de Fomento de la Produccion of Chile, the Industrial Development Corporation of South Africa and the Commonwealth Development Finance Company of the United Kingdom, for example, have prepared brochures suggesting the type of information to be supplied. If the bank decides to go further on the basis of an initial reply, applicants are asked to complete a special questionnaire, tailored to the specific project.

The Industrial Finance Corporation of India uses a two-part ques-

---

[1] These agencies are the Economic Development Administration, the source of much technical assistance, and the Office of Industrial Tax Exemption.

tionnaire. It asks all applicants to complete the generalized first part. Only those whose projects appear worthy of further examination are asked to reply to the more detailed second part, which includes special sections for particular industries. The bank has found this procedure expeditious and satisfactory.

Some banks use branch office staff to review, confirm, or supplement information provided by applicants; at least one small bank has even called upon members of its own board for this purpose.

As a rule bank staff prepare reports dealing in more or less detail with the economic, financial, managerial and legal aspects of the project. The report is then submitted to the principal executive officer, who in turn makes a recommendation to the board of directors (unless he has authority to take final action for the board). The practice of the Industrial Development Corporation of South Africa, of assigning a group of staff members from different departments to investigate and report on applications, has been mentioned earlier.

The Industrial Finance Corporation of India, which has no technical staff, has established five advisory committees, for textiles, sugar, engineering, chemicals and miscellaneous industries. Each committee is composed of two or three experts from the particular industry, two or three government experts, one or two directors of the bank and its chairman. The committees meet regularly to sift applications on the basis of a memorandum prepared by the staff of the bank's head office. Committee members are given the results of all previous investigations of the operations of applicant enterprises in the case of existing concerns. They are also given detailed analyses of the technical and financial aspects of the project, and this is often supplemented by technical advice from government departments. The advisory committee's recommendations are submitted to a committee of the board, which approves or rejects the application or suggests appropriate modifications in the project. Loans for more than a prescribed amount (at the discretion of the board) are reserved for final approval by the full board.

Technical Personnel

The work of appraising applications, investigating projects and undertaking loan supervision requires the services of various kinds of specialists: economists, financial analysts, engineers and lawyers. Some banks have tried to staff themselves with technical personnel; some have made other arrangements for technical services for themselves as well as their clients.

Starting with a minimum of technical staff, until the volume of business builds up, avoids having idle personnel, although it may at the same time limit the amount of business the bank can effectively handle. In many instances the only available technicians are foreign, with relatively high salary demands which would add greatly to administrative expenses. It is often difficult in any case to build up a large technical staff; the banks must compete with private industry for scarce technical skills and may often find themselves unable to offer equally high salaries.

This is particularly a problem for public institutions, even those which may fix salaries without regard to civil service regulations. The relatively lower pay which they offer not only makes it harder for them to recruit technicians, but encourages employees to transfer to private industry after being trained by the bank. The banks tend to accept this situation philosophically, regarding it as one of their contributions to the development of private industry. Nacional Financiera of Mexico tries to reduce salary discrepancies by permitting employees assigned to loan supervision to retain the fees charged for this service. Assignments are rotated to give the greatest number of employees an opportunity thus to supplement their salaries.

At least one private bank, the Industrial Development Bank of Turkey (IDB), finds that the salaries it offers are sufficiently high to be a factor in attracting technical personnel from government service. Whether for this or other reasons, the IDB has been able to build up so large a technical staff, particularly in the engineering and accounting fields, that, as noted earlier, it is able to offer technical assistance even to non-clients, on a fee basis.

By and large, however, banks find it difficult to recruit engineers, accountants and economists. They try to meet the shortage of skills in several ways. The Industrial Development Corporation of South Africa, as noted earlier, gives special training to employees. The Banco Nacional do Desenvolvimento Economico of Brazil arranges special courses for selected personnel. The Instituto de Fomento Nacional of Nicaragua offers scholarships for study abroad. Staff of the Industrial Finance Corporation of India have lectured to university students of business administration on industrial financing. The bank also trains junior staff for the State Finance Corporations, which assist small industry. The Caisse Centrale of France trains African staff by selecting some of those studying at universities in metropolitan France, and giving them an opportunity to gain experience, with limited responsibility, in its offices.

Sometimes a bank can arrange to have access to technical services without building up a technical staff of its own. The Pakistan Industrial Credit and Investment Corporation and the Development Finance Corporation of Ceylon, and their clients, rely heavily on public organizations for technical services. The Puerto Rico Industrial Development Company draws on very extensive assistance offered by the Economic Development Administration in reviewing applications, undertaking investigations and giving advice when enterprises fall into difficulties. The Corporacion de Fomento de la Produccion of Chile, although well-staffed with technicians, calls upon various state institutions, private associations and universities for economic research and advice on specific technical problems. The Industrial Finance Corporation of India seeks advice from various government departments and the members of the advisory committees described earlier; in special cases it employs independent private experts for surveys and reports.

International organizations are another source of technical advice. The International Labour Organisation, the Food and Agriculture Organization, the U.N. Technical Assistance Administration and the International Bank have all made available the services of one or more staff members from time to time. National financial institutions may likewise be in a position to help; the assistance pro-

vided by the Herstelbank in the Netherlands to the Development
Bank of Ethiopia indicates what may be done.

Some banks have turned to private consultants. The Pakistan
Industrial Credit and Investment Corporation sometimes engages
consultants for project appraisals. The Government Development
Bank for Puerto Rico occasionally calls in private firms for economic
appraisals or engineering studies; the Development Finance Corporation of Ceylon employs licensed appraisers for property valua-
tions; and the Banco Nacional do Desenvolvimento Economico of
Brazil engages engineers to supervise construction.

Arrangements for compensating experts vary. In the case of
investments of the International Finance Corporation the investment enterprise is normally expected to assume the cost of outside
consultants (including local counsel) in connection with the project.
The Industrial Finance Corporation of India requires a deposit from
applicants to cover the cost of investigation. It refunds the deposit
if it agrees to lend; the deposit is forfeited if the application is
rejected. Still a third approach is that of the Government Development Bank for Puerto Rico and the Commonwealth Development
Finance Company of the United Kingdom, which charge applicants
for any investigation made by outside consultants, irrespective of
the ultimate decision on the application. Where consultants are engaged for loan supervision, rather than investigation or analysis of
applications prior to an investment decision, it is general practice
to charge the client.

THE ENTIRE EXPERIENCE of development banks has been gained
within a short span of years and, as far as the private banks are
concerned, by a very few institutions. Policies and practices are for
the most part still in an experimental stage; many will be modified,
some will be abandoned. Just as no single model of development
bank is suitable to all countries, so no single solution to a particular
problem has been found appropriate by all banks. And the purposes
or economic settings of many new banks may well be markedly
unlike those of existing banks. These new banks will be confronted

with new problems and the need to devise new solutions for old difficulties.

For all these reasons, this book has not intended to imply that any single way is the best or the correct way for the sponsors of a bank or its management to proceed. The objective has rather been to describe how a number of problems of common concern have thus far been dealt with by a variety of banks, and to set forth the considerations which lie behind the differences in procedure. This recital of experience and reasoning may, it is hoped, prove useful to existing and future banks alike. Existing banks may draw from it suggestions for fresh and more effective approaches to familiar issues; new banks may find in it precedents readily adaptable to new contexts.

Appendix

APPENDIX A

Data on Development Banks[1]

Country	City	Bank	Form of Financing Extended		Ownership[2]
			Loan	Equity Investment	
Argentina	Buenos Aires	Industrial Bank	X		
Belgian Congo	Leopoldville	Agricultural and Industrial Credit Corporation	X		mixed; majority public
Brazil	Rio de Janeiro	National Development Bank	X		
British Guiana	Georgetown	Credit Corporation	X		
Burma	Rangoon	Industrial Development Corporation	X	X	
Ceylon	Colombo	State Mortgage Bank	X		
Ceylon	Colombo	Agricultural and Industrial Credit Corporation	X		
	Colombo	Development Finance Corporation	X	X	private
Chile	Santiago	Development Corporation	X	X	
China	Taipei, Taiwan	Development Corporation	X	X	mixed; majority private
Cuba	Havana	Agricultural and Industrial Development Bank	X	X	
	Havana	Economic and Social Development Bank	X	X	
Ecuador	Quito	National Development Bank	X		
El Salvador	San Salvador	Development Institute	X	X	

Country	City	Bank	Loan	Equity Investment	Ownership[2]
Ethiopia	Addis Ababa	Development Bank	X	X	
Federation of Rhodesia and Nyasaland	Lusaka	Northern Rhodesia Industrial Loans Board	X		
Ghana	Accra	Industrial Development Corporation	X	X	
Greece	Athens	Economic Development Financing Organization	X	X	
	Athens	National Mortgage Bank	X		
Guatemala	Guatemala City	Development Institute	X		
Haiti	Port-au-Prince	Agricultural and Industrial Credit Institute	X	X	
Honduras	Tegucigalpa	National Development Bank	X		
Iceland	Reykjavik	Bank of Development	X		
India	Bombay	Industrial Credit and Investment Corporation	X	X	private
	New Delhi	Industrial Finance Corporation	X		mixed; majority public
	New Delhi	National Industrial Development Corporation	X	X	
		State Financial Corporations	X		mixed; majority public
Indonesia	Djakarta	Industrial Development Bank	X		
	Djakarta	Development Bank of Indonesia	X	X	
Iran	Tehran	Industrial Credit Bank	X	X	
	Tehran	Industrial and Mining Development Bank	X	X	private
Iraq	Baghdad	Industrial Bank	X	X	
Ireland	Dublin	Industrial Credit Company	X	X	mixed; majority public
Israel	Tel Aviv	Industrial Development Bank	X	X	mixed; majority private

Country	City	Bank	Loan	Equity Investment	Ownership[2]
Jamaica	Kingston	Small Business Loan Board	X		
	Kingston	Industrial Development Corporation	X	X	
Japan	Tokyo	Development Bank	X		
Jordan	Amman	Development Bank	X	X	mixed; majority public
Korea	Seoul	Reconstruction Bank	X		
Lebanon	Beirut	Agricultural, Industrial and Real Estate Credit Bank	X		mixed; majority private
Malaya	Kuala Lumpur	Industrial Development (Finance) Corporation	X	X	mixed; majority private
Mexico	Mexico, D.F.	National Investment Bank (Nacional Financiera)	X	X	mixed; majority public
Morocco	Rabat	National Bank for Economic Development	X	X	mixed; majority public
Nicaragua	Managua	National Development Institute	X		
Nigeria	Lagos	Federal Loans Board	X		
	Kaduna	Northern Regional Development Corporation		X	
	Enugu	Eastern Region Development Corporation	X	X	
	Ibadan	Western Region Finance Corporation	X	X	
	Victoria, Cameroons	Southern Cameroons Production Development Board	X		
Pakistan	Karachi	Industrial Finance Corporation	X		mixed; majority public
	Karachi	Industrial Credit and Investment Corporation	X	X	private
Peru	Lima	Industrial Bank	X		mixed; majority public
Philippines	Manila	National Development Company		X	
	Manila	Development Bank	X		

Country	City	Bank	Loan	Equity Investment	Ownership[2]
	Manila	Industrial Development Center	X		
Puerto Rico	San Juan	Industrial Development Company	X	X	
	San Juan	Government Development Bank	X		
Singapore	Singapore	Industrial Promotion Board	X	X	
Thailand	Bangkok	Industrial Finance Corporation	X	X	private
Trinidad and Tobago	Port of Spain, Trinidad	Industrial Development Corporation	X	X	
Tunisia	Tunis	National Investment Corporation		X	mixed; majority public
Turkey	Istanbul	Industrial Development Bank	X	X	private
Uganda	Kampala	Development Corporation	X	X	
Union of South Africa	Johannesburg	Industrial Development Corporation	X	X	
	Johannesburg	Industrial Finance Corporation	X	X	mixed; majority private
United Arab Republic					
Egypt	Cairo	Industrial Bank	X	X	mixed; majority public
Syria	Damascus	Industrial Bank	X	X	mixed; majority private
Venezuela	Caracas	Development Corporation	X	X	
Viet-Nam	Saigon	Industrial Development Center	X		
Yugoslavia	Belgrade	Investment Bank	X		

Form of Financing Extended

[1] The listing does not include institutions in the highly industrialized countries of Western Europe, in the United States, Canada, and Australia, or in countries which are not members of the International Bank.

[2] Wholly government-owned, unless otherwise indicated.

Sample Loan Agreement Provisions[1]

Commitment Charge

[1]   As from the ———————————————— the Borrower shall pay to PICIC a commitment charge at the rate of ————% per annum on the principal amount of the loan not withdrawn by the Borrower from time to time. The commitment charge shall become due and payable on the 1st of January, 1st of April, 1st of July and 1st of October in each year and shall be calculated on the highest amount of loan standing to the credit of the Borrower during the three months preceding the date on which the charge becomes due and payable.

Pakistan Industrial Credit & Investment Corporation Limited

[2]   From the date of coming into force of these Heads of Agreement (as defined in Clause IX hereof), the Borrower shall pay to ICICI in U.S. $ a Commitment Charge at the rate of 1% per annum on the amount of the Loan undrawn from time to time. This will be calculated half-yearly and will be payable on the same dates as are given in sub-clause 8 above.

Industrial Credit and Investment Corporation of India

[1] These provisions are set forth for illustrative purposes only. It is not suggested that any one of them would necessarily be appropriate, without modification, to any other bank. Each has been drafted not only with the purposes of a particular bank in mind, but against the background of the laws and practices of a particular country.

Prepayment

[1] The Borrower will have the option to repay in whole or in part any of the installments referred to above before their due date, subject to —

a) The payment of a premium calculated at the percentages specified below (actual and not per annum) on the amount earlier repaid:—

Time of Repayment	*Premium*
Not more than 6 years before due date	½%
More than 5 years but not more than 10 years before due date	1%
More than 10 years before due date	2%

b) Prior notice in writing to ICICI of not less than 90 days, of the intention to repay in advance of the due date, stating the amount and proposed earlier date of repayment.

Except as ICICI and the Borrower shall otherwise agree any such repayment shall be applied to the several maturities of [such part of] the principal amount of the Loan in inverse order of maturity.

Provided however that the Borrower shall not be entitled to exercise the rights of earlier repayment set out above, unless and until the Government of India have consented to the earlier repayment of the corresponding obligations undertaken by ICICI towards IBRD in terms of ICICI's Loan Agreement with IBRD. ICICI undertakes to apply to the Government of India at the appropriate time for such consent whenever the Borrower informs ICICI that it is desired to exercise such rights of earlier repayment.

Industrial Credit and Investment Corporation of India

[2] Unless otherwise agreed between the parties the Borrower shall not have right to prepay either the entire loan or any installment thereof.

Pakistan Industrial Credit & Investment Corporation

[3] The Borrower is entitled upon not less than sixty days' prior notice by registered letter to prepay all or part of the Loan. Every partial prepayment shall include one or more installments of principal. Prepayment shall only be permitted when all due payments of interest and

principal have been entirely paid and at the same time the following premiums on prepayment are paid. The premium for prepayment shall be as follows: Prepayment less than 3 years before maturity .. ½% on the amount prepaid, more than 3 but less than 6 years before maturity .. 1%, more than 6 but less than 11 years before maturity .. 2%, more than 11 but less than 14 years before maturity .. 3%, more than 14 but less than 16 years before maturity .. 4%, more than 16 years before maturity .. 5%. In special cases Investitionskredit may waive payment of the premium, but the Borrower has no legal claim to such a waiver.

Partial prepayment shall be applied to the several installments of the Loan in inverse order of their maturity.

(unofficial translation)
Austrian Investment Credit Corporation

Use of Loan Proceeds

[1]   The Borrower undertakes to use the proceeds of the Loan solely for the purposes described in sub-clause 1 above and further undertakes that the goods purchased with the proceeds of the Loan shall be used exclusively in the carrying out of the project.

If, for any reason, the Borrower shall find itself unable to comply with the requirements of sub-clause 3 above it shall immediately inform ICICI.

No part of the proceeds of the Loan shall be made on account of expenditure in Rupees or goods acquired from sources within India, nor can the proceeds be used to finance goods from countries which are not Members of the IBRD, except Switzerland.

Except with the consent in writing of ICICI first sought and obtained, the Borrower shall not use the proceeds of the Loan for the purpose of acquiring any other currency.

(Other clauses, as required)
Industrial Credit and Investment Corporation of India

[2]   (a) The Borrower/s shall apply the proceeds of the loan exclusively to financing the cost of goods and services required to carry out the Project hereinabove described. Foreign currency shall be disbursed only for goods and services that have neither been paid in Pakistan Rupees nor were produced in or, in the case of services, sup-

plied from Pakistan. The specific goods and services to be financed out of the proceeds of the Loan provided for herein shall be determined by agreement between PICIC and the Borrower/s, subject to modification by further agreement between them.

(b) No disbursements of foreign currency shall be made against expenditures in territories of Pakistan or of any country, except Switzer-land, which is not a member of the IBRD or for goods produced in including services supplied from such countries.

OR

No disbursement of foreign currency shall be made if goods are purchased or services supplied from sources other than those specified in Code 99 of the International Cooperation Administration Geographic Code Book as in effect at the time the goods are finally ordered or the services supplied.

Pakistan Industrial Credit & Investment Corporation

Future Transactions of Borrower

[1] Except with the consent of ICICI, which will not be unreasonably withheld, the Borrower shall not —

a) Acquire shares in, make any loan to, or give any guarantee or credit (other than normal trade credit and deposits on call of funds in excess of day to day requirements) to or for any Company or person.

b) Sell its undertaking or dispose of any of its freehold or leasehold property, or (except in the ordinary course of business) part with any of its other Assets.

The Borrower will not, except with the prior consent of ICICI which will not be unreasonably withheld, raise any loan, issue any loan capital, issue any equity or preference capital, change the capital structure of the Borrower, create any charge or give any guarantee except that it may —

a) Give normal trade guarantees or make temporary loans or advances to staff, to contractors or suppliers, in the ordinary course of its business.

b) Obtain from a Bank or Banks overdraft or other facilities against the security referred to in Clause V (10) above.

Except with the consent of ICICI the Borrower will not change its practice with regard to remuneration of Directors, whether by means of ordinary remuneration or commission.

The Borrower shall not change its Memorandum and Articles of Association without the prior consent of ICICI.

The Directors shall not dispose of their shareholdings in the Borrower without the prior consent of ICICI.

Industrial Credit and Investment Corporation of India

[2] Except with the previous consent in writing of PICIC the Borrower/s shall not incur, guarantee or assume any debt, or create any mortgage or charge or other encumbrance on its properties provided, however, the Borrower/s can:—

(a) give normal trade guarantee in the ordinary course of business; and

(b) obtain from its bankers overdraft or other facilities in accordance with the provisions of paragraph 6 of Article IV hereof.

Except with the previous consent in writing of PICIC which will not be unreasonably withheld, the Borrower/s will not:—

(a) acquire shares in make any loan to or give credit (other than normal trade credit and deposits on call of funds in excess of day to day requirement) to or for any Company or person;

(b) sell the undertakings of the Borrower/s or any of its freehold or leasehold property or, (except in the ordinary course of business) part with any other of its assets;

(c) lease, transfer, let-out, sub-let, alienate or otherwise dispose of any of its properties [proposed to be mortgaged or charged to PICIC];

(d) enter into any hire purchase agreement as Purchaser;

(e) enter into any transaction or series of transactions whereby it may receive less than the full ex-works commercial price of the products of its factory (subject to normal trade discounts);

(f) except as otherwise provided herein issue any shares in the capital of the company of whatever class or in any manner change its capital structure.

Without the previous consent in writing of PICIC the Borrower/s shall not declare any dividend.

Without prior approval of PICIC the Borrower/s shall not change its Memorandum or Articles of Association or its Managing Agency Agreement or the remuneration paid to its Directors and Managing

Agents, and shall not undertake any amalgamation, reconstruction, consolidation or winding up.

Pakistan Industrial Credit & Investment Corporation

Information and Inspection

[1] The Borrower will keep in close touch with ICICI on the progress of its business both during the period of construction of the Project and subsequently.

a) To this end the Borrower agrees that ICICI and IBRD may inspect the goods purchased out of the Loan and the sites, works, etc., involved in the Project during the period of its construction and may also inspect the plant, installations, equipment, etc., during its operation. The costs of such inspection and the out-of-pocket expenses incurred by the officers of ICICI during such inspection will be paid by the Borrower.

b) The Borrower shall maintain records showing the use of the goods financed with the Loan, the progress and cost of the Project and the operations and financial condition of the Borrower. Such records shall be open to examination by ICICI and any authorised representative of IBRD.

c) The Borrower shall provide to ICICI all such information relating to the Project and its operations as ICICI shall from time to time at its discretion request including information relating to the financial condition of the Borrower.

d) The Borrower will inform ICICI promptly of the happening of any event likely to have a substantial effect on the Borrower's profits or business; if for instance there are delays during the construction of the Project as provided to ICICI or if after the Project has been completed the monthly production or sales are quite different from the ordinary run, the Borrower will inform ICICI accordingly with an explanation of the reasons.

e) The Borrower will allow any whole-time officer of ICICI or a qualified practising Auditor to examine its books and papers at the Borrower's Registered Office and will give all facilities to enable any technically qualified person chosen by ICICI to report on the business of the Borrower at any time. The out-of-pocket expenses of such officer and the expenses and fees of such Auditor or technically qualified person will be paid by the Borrower.

Provided that if the technically qualified person is not a whole-time employee of ICICI such technically qualified person shall be acceptable to the Borrower having regard to his other activities, if any.

Industrial Credit and Investment Corporation of India

[2] The Borrower/s shall maintain books, accounts and records adequate to identify the goods and services financed out of the proceeds of the Loan, to disclose the use thereof in the Project, to record the progress of the Project (including the cost thereof) and to reflect in accordance with consistently maintained sound accounting practices the operations and financial condition of the Borrower/s.

The Borrower/s shall enable authorised representatives of PICIC, IBRD and/or DLF to inspect the sites, works and construction included in the Project, and any other properties or equipment owned or operated by the Borrower/s; to examine or audit any books, accounts, records, contracts, orders, invoices, studies, reports or other documents relating to expenditures for the Project or to the progress of construction, maintenance and results of operation of the Project or otherwise to the operations and financial condition of the Borrower/s. The travelling and out of pocket expenses of the representatives of PICIC incurred in such inspection shall be paid by the Borrower/s.

The Borrower/s shall furnish to PICIC, IBRD and/or DLF all such information at such times in such form and in such detail as PICIC, IBRD and/or DLF shall reasonably request, concerning the expenditures of the proceeds of the loan, the progress of the Project, the goods and services, and the operations and financial condition of the Borrower/s.

Such information shall include (a) yearly audited balance sheets and statements of profit and loss account of the Borrower/s certified by independent accountants satisfactory to PICIC, IBRD and/or DLF whose fees and expenses shall be for the account of the Borrower/s; (b) quarterly financial statements of expenditures on the Project in a form prescribed by PICIC.

Pakistan Industrial Credit & Investment Corporation

Accounts

[1] The Borrower will keep proper books and accounts and will not radically change its accounting system without prior notice to ICICI.

Industrial Credit and Investment Corporation of India

[2]   The Borrower/s shall appoint and keep appointed a Registered Accountant acceptable to PICIC as its Auditor.

The Borrower/s will not change its bankers or auditor without the prior written consent of PICIC.

The Borrower/s will keep proper books of accounts and will not change the accounting system of the Borrower/s without prior notice to PICIC.

Pakistan Industrial Credit & Investment Corporation

Costs

[1]   All costs, charges and expenses (including charges of the legal advisers of ICICI) in any way incurred by ICICI in connection with or relating to this transaction including investigation of title to the immovable properties if necessary, preparation and stamping of the documents required and expenses incurred by ICICI in seeking approval of the loan by IBRD shall be borne and paid by the Borrower.

Industrial Credit and Investment Corporation of India

[2]   All specific costs, charges, and expenses (including cost of legal advisers of PICIC) in any way incurred by PICIC in connection with or relating to this transaction including investigation of title to immovable properties, preparation, execution, stamping and registration of the documents required as security for the loan will be borne by the Borrower/s.

Pakistan Industrial Credit & Investment Corporation

[3]   Charges of all kinds payable by Investitionskredit to third parties and necessary or useful for the administration of the Loan shall be reimbursed to Investitionskredit by the Borrower immediately upon written notice.

The foregoing provision also applies to all charges falling upon Investitionskredit and arising out of the failure or delay in performance or incomplete performance of any obligation under this Loan Agreement.

(unofficial translation)
Austrian Investment Credit Corporation

Security

[1]   The Loan is to be secured by:—

(a) a first legal mortgage on the Borrower's present and future immovable properties wherever situated including all buildings, fixed plants, machinery and fixtures (including trade fixtures) thereon;

(b) a first floating charge on all other assets of the Borrower (subject only to the hypothecation or charge in favour of the Borrower's bankers referred to in paragraph 6 hereof);

(c) a hypothecation and a trust receipt in respect of all movable machinery;

(d) a demand promissory note for the amount of the loan executed jointly and severally by the Borrower and all its Directors, renewable every three years. Provided that the Borrower shall at any time at the request of PICIC issue usance bill or bills in favour of PICIC in lieu of the demand promissory note in amounts and maturities corresponding to all or any instalment fixed under paragraph 8 of Article I and outstanding on the date of issue of such usance bill or bills;

(e) a personal guarantee executed jointly and severally by all the Directors of the Borrower undertaking to repay the Loan as if they were the principal debtors; and

(f) assignment by the Borrower by way of mortgage of the benefit of its contracts with the suppliers of goods to be imported under this Agreement.

The Borrower hereby agrees, undertakes and covenants to execute the legal mortgage in respect of the immovable properties forming the security for the loan, containing such terms and conditions and stipulations including the powers of sale as PICIC may determine and such other letters of hypothecation and/or pledge and charge, agreements of guarantee and indemnity and all other documents as may be required by PICIC and to register such of the above documents as require registration under law at their sole cost and expense.

PICIC shall have the right to transfer or assign the Deed of Mortgage at its absolute discretion.

Pending completion, execution and registration of the Mortgage Deed referred to in sub-para 1(a) above the Borrower shall:—

(i) create in favour of PICIC an equitable mortgage of the Borrower's immovable properties present and future as and when acquired by deposit of title deeds with PICIC; and

(ii) execute a Power of Attorney in favour of PICIC giving PICIC full powers to execute, record, register and file as Attorney for the Borrower/s the Deed of Legal Mortgage referred to in para 1(a) at any time it considers appropriate and in the appropriate jurisdiction or offices.

Pakistan Industrial Credit & Investment Corporation

Insurance

[1]   The Borrower undertakes that proper and adequate arrangements will be made for the insurance against usual risks of all the goods to be imported for the purpose of the Project whether financed out of the proceeds of the Loan or not [and in particular undertakes that the goods to be financed out of the proceeds of the Loan will be insured against all marine risk for their purchase value in the currency in which such goods are paid for].

Industrial Credit and Investment Corporation of India

[2]   The Borrower/s shall take out and maintain such insurance against such risks, in such amounts and in such manner as shall be consistent with sound commercial practice and as shall be required by PICIC. It will regularly pay the premia due till the loan is fully paid off and assign the policies in favour of PICIC and deposit the same with PICIC. It is agreed that if the Borrower/s fails to effect insurance or pay the premia on due dates PICIC shall have the right to effect insurance, and/or pay the premium on behalf of the Borrower/s and treat the sums so paid as additions to the principal sums due.

Pakistan Industrial Credit & Investment Corporation

[3]   The Borrower shall at all times maintain adequate fire insurance on its buildings of all kinds, its machinery, installations, tools, operating and business equipment, raw materials and supplies, semi-finished products and finished products, and goods, on the basis of the original cost thereof, and shall inform Investitionskredit thereof. At the request of Investitionskredit, provision shall be made for payment of the insurance monies to Investitionskredit insofar as the insurance concerns goods for whose production or acquisition the Loan was granted or which were given as security for the Loan. If the Borrower should fail

to pay its insurance premiums when due Investitionskredit shall be entitled to pay the same. The Borrower shall immediately reimburse Investitionskredit therefor.

The Borrower shall inform Investitionskredit of all other insurance taken out; on request of Investitionskredit the Borrower shall take out and maintain such insurance, against such risks and in such amounts, as shall be consistent with sound business practice and shall inform Investitionskredit of the execution of such request.

(unofficial translation)
Austrian Investment Credit Corporation

Representations (Selected)

[1] The Borrower states that it has taken all practicable steps to obtain all the necessary assurances regarding availability of raw materials, transport, power, water and all other facilities necessary in order to carry out the project for which the facilities are granted.

The Borrower has produced to ICICI the requisite permissions under the Foreign Exchange Regulation Act—

a) for the Borrower to raise the loan which is the subject of these Heads of Agreement and to undertake the repayment and other obligations herein set out;

and

(other permissions if necessary)

The Borrower has obtained and exhibited to ICICI letters from the Government of India indicating that Government will issue the necessary Import Licences covering the import of that part of the capital equipment to be financed out of the Loan when ICICI notifies Government that the loan project has been approved by the IBRD for the purposes of a withdrawal from loan granted by the IBRD to ICICI.

The Borrower states that when the Import Licences referred to in the preceding paragraph have been received it will be possessed of Import Licences covering all the imported capital equipment needed for the purpose referred to in Clause II above.

Industrial Credit and Investment Corporation of India

[2] That all governmental and other necessary licences, approvals or consents for implementation of the Project, the accomplishment of the

purposes of the financing and the execution and delivery of this Agreement and the obligations to be performed thereunder have been obtained.

The Borrower/s shall have satisfied PICIC that it has made satisfactory arrangements to engage competent technical staff to run and operate the Project.

Pakistan Industrial Credit & Investment Corporation

Maintenance of Facilities

[1] The Borrower/s will during the subsistence of the Loan, keep its buildings, machinery, plants, fittings, implements and other effects present and future in good repair and proper working condition.

Pakistan Industrial Credit & Investment Corporation

Statement of Operational Policy

(a) The Company will not seek in any enterprise financed by it a controlling interest or any other interest which would give it primary responsibility for the management of such enterprise. The Company will to the maximum extent possible, consistent with the protection of its interests, and after satisfying itself that qualified and experienced management is and will continue to be available, leave the management and control in the hands of the enterprise so financed.

(b) With the exception of intermediate investment of its liquid funds in short-term securities, the Company will keep its financing, whether through loans or equity participations or guarantees, diversified, both as to types of undertakings and as to location. Normally it will not commit more than 5% of the total of its original paid-up share capital and Government investment to any single undertaking but may go up to 10% in exceptional circumstances.

(c) The Company normally will revolve its funds by selling its investments at its discretion whenever it can receive a fair price therefor. In selling such investments the Company will pay due regard both to its own interests and to those of other participants in the particular investment.

(d) The Company will build reserves consistent with sound financial practices. (The application to the reserves of the net profits of the Company, after provision for taxes and other appropriate reserves, is provided for in Article 154 of the Company's Articles of Association.)

(e) The Directors will use their powers to prevent any one person or company or group of affiliated persons or companies obtaining effective control of the Company.

Pakistan Industrial Credit & Investment Corporation

Sample Charters

APPENDIX D-1

An Act to provide for the establishment of the Development Finance Corporation of Ceylon and for matters connected therewith.

[Date of Assent: October 4, 1955]

Be it enacted by the Queen's Most Excellent Majesty, by and with the advice and consent of the Senate and the House of Representatives of Ceylon in this present Parliament assembled, and by the authority of the same, as follows:

1. This Act may be cited as the Development Finance Corporation of Ceylon Act, No. 35 of 1955.

2. (1) There shall be established, in accordance with the provisions of this Act, a corporation (hereinafter referred to as the "Corporation") which—

(a) shall, until there are shareholders of the Corporation, consist of the Directors for the time being of the Corporation, and shall, when there are such shareholders, consist of the Directors and the shareholders for the time being of the Corporation, and

(b) shall be called the Development Finance Corporation of Ceylon.

(2) The head office of the Corporation shall be in Colombo. Such branch offices of the Corporation as the Board of Directors may consider necessary may be established in places in Ceylon other than Colombo.

3. The Corporation shall in the name assigned to it by section 2 be a body corporate and shall have perpetual succession and a common seal and may sue and be sued in such name.

4. (1) The purposes of the Corporation shall be—

(a) to assist in the establishment, expansion and modernization of private industrial and agricultural enterprises in Ceylon, and

(b) to encourage and promote the participation of private capital, both internal and external, in such enterprises.

(2) Any industrial or agricultural enterprise in Ceylon in which the Government holds not more than 20% of the capital shall, for the purposes of paragraph (a) of sub-section (1) be deemed to be a private industrial or agricultural enterprise in Ceylon.

5. In carrying out its purposes, the Corporation may exercise all or any of the following powers:

(i) provide finance in the form of long-term or medium-term loans with or without security, or by purchasing or subscribing for shares or other securities, or by acquiring any other interest;

(ii) underwrite new issues of stocks, shares, bonds, debentures and other securities;

(iii) guarantee loans from other private investment sources;

(iv) make funds available for re-investment by selling any investments of the Corporation when and as appropriate;

(v) borrow funds for the purposes of the business of the Corporation from sources either in Ceylon or abroad and give security for any loans obtained;

(vi) furnish managerial, technical and administrative advice and assist in obtaining managerial, technical and administrative services to private industrial and agricultural enterprises in Ceylon;

(vii) invest idle funds and reserves of the Corporation in appropriate securities;

(viii) acquire, hold, take or give on lease or hire mortgage, pledge and sell or otherwise dispose of any immovable or movable property;

(ix) accept, before the date on which it is due, any payment in respect of a loan granted by the Corporation;

(x) open deposit accounts with any bank;

(xi) draw, accept, or endorse bills of exchange for the purposes of the business of the Corporation;

(xii) give any guarantee or indemnity to, and enter into any arrangements with, the Government, any local authority, or any body corporate or other person, in order to obtain any rights, concessions and privileges that may seem to the Corporation to be conducive to any object of the Corporation;

(xiii) make appropriate provision for the welfare of employees or ex-employees of the Corporation and of their dependents; and

(xiv) do all such other things as are incident or conducive to the attainment of its purposes.

6. The liability of any shareholder shall be limited to the amount, if any, unpaid on his shares.

7. (1) The authorized share capital of the Corporation shall be eight million rupees divided into eighty thousand ordinary shares of one hundred rupees each.

(2) The Corporation shall offer the shares referred to in sub-section (1) to the public for subscription at such time or times, in such amount or amounts and in such manner as the Corporation may determine, and shall allot such shares.

8. The Corporation shall not transact any business until at least sixty thousand of the shares referred to in section 7 have been fully subscribed and allotted.

9. (1) The general supervision, control and administration of the affairs and business of the Corporation shall be vested in a Board of Directors constituted in accordance with section 10.

(2) The Board of Directors may exercise all the powers and do all the acts which may be exercised or done by the Corporation.

(3) The Board of Directors may utilise the funds of the Corporation for the purpose of defraying any expenditure incurred in the management of the affairs of the Corporation, the transaction of the business of the Corporation, the remuneration of the Directors and employees of the Corporation, and the exercise of the powers and the performance of the duties of such Board under this Act.

(4) It shall be the duty of the Board of Directors to ensure that every application dealt with on behalf of the Corporation is considered strictly on its financial and economic merits irrespective of all other considerations.

(5) The Board of Directors shall take all such measures as may be necessary to ensure that any financial assistance rendered by the Corporation to any private industrial or agricultural enterprise is utilised for the purpose for which it is given.

(6) The Corporation shall not make an investment in or otherwise transact business with an enterprise in which a Director of the Corporation is a partner, director or shareholder, or is in any other way directly or indirectly interested, unless the transaction is unanimously approved by the other Directors of the Corporation.

(7) The Board of Directors shall appoint a General Manager of the Corporation, and he shall, subject to the direction of the Board of Directors, be the chief executive officer of the Corporation.

10. (1) The Board of Directors shall be constituted in accordance with the provisions of this section.

(2) So long as there is outstanding any loan made by the Government to the Corporation pursuant to the provisions of this Act, the Minister of Finance, acting in consultation with the Minister of Industries, Housing and Social Services, shall be entitled from time to time to appoint one person as a Director (hereinafter called the "Government Director") of the Corporation, to remove such person from office and, on a vacancy being caused in such office whether by resignation, death, removal or otherwise, to appoint a Director to fill the vacancy. The Government Director shall not be liable to retire by rotation or be removed from office except by the Minister of Finance as aforesaid and shall not be bound to hold any qualification shares. Subject as aforesaid the Government Director shall be entitled to the same rights and privileges and be subject to the same obligations as any other Director of the Corporation, except that, if the Government Director is a public servant, he shall not be entitled to any remuneration as such Director.

(3) The following shall be *ex-officio* Directors of the Corporation without the right to vote:

(a) The holder for the time being of the office of Director of the Ceylon Institute of Scientific and Industrial Research.

(b) The holder for the time being of the office of General Manager of the Corporation.

The *ex-officio* members shall not be required to hold any qualification shares.

(4) There shall be not less than four and not more than six other directors (hereinafter referred to as "Shareholder Directors"). The Minister of Finance shall appoint the initial Shareholder Directors. At the end of each financial year of the Corporation after the Corporation is entitled to transact business, one of the initial Shareholder Directors

so appointed shall retire. The Director who shall so retire shall be determined by the drawing of lots. Any successor to an initial Shareholder Director who retires pursuant to this sub-section or whose office becomes vacant for any other cause and any new Shareholder Director shall be elected and hold office in accordance with the regulations of the Corporation made under section 11. An initial Shareholder Director shall be eligible to be elected to succeed himself if qualified to be elected under sub-section (5). A majority of the Shareholder Directors shall at all times be citizens of Ceylon.

(5) A person shall be qualified to be elected and hold office as a Shareholder Director if and so long as he—

(a) has, or is an officer, director or partner of a company or partnership which has, shares of the par value of not less than five thousand rupees in the capital of the Corporation,

(b) is not a Senator or a Member of Parliament or a member of a local authority,

(c) is not a paid employee of the Corporation,

(d) is not a person who, having been declared an insolvent or a bankrupt under any law in force in Ceylon or in any other country, is an undischarged insolvent or bankrupt,

(e) is not found or declared to be of unsound mind under any law in force in Ceylon or in any other country, and

(f) is not serving a sentence of imprisonment imposed by any court in Ceylon or in any other country.

Provided, however, that the initial Shareholder Directors shall not be required to have the qualification specified in paragraph (a) of this sub-section until two months have elapsed after the first issue of shares.

(6) The members of the Board of Directors shall elect one of the Shareholder Directors to be the Chairman of the Board of Directors.

11. (1) The Board of Directors shall forthwith after the commencement of this Act make regulations dealing with those matters not provided for by this Act which, in the case of a company formed under the Companies Ordinance, No. 51 of 1938, would be dealt with in the Articles of Association.

(2) Subject to the provisions of this Act, the shareholders may by special resolution amend or rescind any regulation made under sub-section (1) or add any fresh regulation to the regulations so made.

In this sub-section, the expression "special resolution" means a resolution passed by a majority of not less than three-fourths of such share-

holders as, being entitled so to do, vote in person or by proxy at a
meeting of the shareholders of which not less than twenty-one days'
notice has been duly given to the shareholders specifying the resolution
intended to be proposed at that meeting.

(3) The regulations made under this section shall be the regulations
of the Corporation in regard to the matters to which they relate.

(4) The regulations of the Corporation shall have the force of law.

12. The provisions of the Companies Ordinance, No. 51 of 1938, shall,
mutatis mutandis, apply to the Corporation in regard to any matter for
which there is no provision in this Act or in any regulation of the
Corporation:

Provided, however, that the Corporation shall not be required to be
registered under such Ordinance nor shall the Registrar of Companies
have any power with respect to the Corporation.

13. (1) For the purposes of its business the Corporation may borrow
from the Government, and the Government may lend to the Corporation from the Consolidated Fund of Ceylon without charging any interest, the sum of sixteen million rupees. Any loan made under this
sub-section shall be repayable to the Government by the Corporation in
fifteen equal annual instalments the first of which shall be due in the
sixteenth year succeeding the year in which such loan is granted by the
Government, but the Corporation shall have the right to prepay all or
any part of any such loan at any time. Every sum in repayment of such
loan shall be paid to the Secretary to the Treasury who shall credit it
to the Consolidated Fund of Ceylon.

(2) So long as there is outstanding any loan made by the Government
to the Corporation under sub-section (1), —

(a) the Corporation shall set aside in each year in a Special Reserve Fund a sum equal to not less than twenty *per centum* of the
net profits of the Corporation as shown in the Corporation's financial
statement for that year, until the amount so set aside equals the
amount of the Government loan then outstanding, and

(b) the Corporation shall not in any year declare or pay dividends
in excess of twelve *per centum* on the share capital of the Corporation.

(3) Amounts set aside in the Special Reserve Fund under sub-section
(2) shall not be used for the business of the Corporation but may be
invested in accordance with the provisions of this Act.

(4) If, while there is outstanding any loan made by the Government
to the Corporation under sub-section (1), the liabilities of the Corpora-

tion (excluding paid-up share capital) exceed the assets of the Corporation by thirty *per centum* or more of the aggregate of the paid-up share
capital of the Corporation and the amount of the Government loan at
the time outstanding, all as determined by the auditors of the Corporation, the Government shall have the right in its discretion to request
the shareholders to replenish the capital and, if the capital is not re-
plenished, to require liquidation of the Corporation.

(5) In the event of the liquidation of the Corporation no payment
shall be made in respect of any debt to the Crown incurred by the
Corporation in pursuance of this section until the amount of the paid-up
share capital is distributed among the shareholders in accordance with
the capital contributed to the Corporation on their shares.

14. (1) The Government is hereby authorized to guarantee, on such
terms and conditions as the Government may determine, loans raised
by the Corporation from the International Bank for Reconstruction and
Development. The loans authorized to be guaranteed under this sub-
section may be denominated in foreign currency. No guarantee shall be
given under this sub-section if the aggregate amount of all loans
guaranteed under this sub-section exceeds, or as a result of the loan to
be guaranteed would exceed, the equivalent of twenty-four million
rupees at the rate of exchange prevailing at the date of the loan agreement to which such guarantee would apply.

(2) All sums payable by the Government under any guarantee given
under sub-section (1) are hereby charged on the Consolidated Fund of
Ceylon.

(3) All sums payable by the Corporation in respect of principal,
interest and other charges on any loan to the Corporation from the International Bank for Reconstruction and Development or by the Government under any guarantee given under sub-section (1) shall, notwithstanding anything to the contrary in any law of Ceylon, be paid—

(a) without deduction for, and free from, any taxes, duties or fees
now or hereafter imposed by or under any law of Ceylon, and

(b) free from all restrictions now or hereafter imposed by or under
any law of Ceylon:

Provided, however, that the preceding provisions of this sub-section
shall not apply to any taxes, duties, fees or restrictions upon payments
under any bond or promissory note to a holder thereof other than the
International Bank for Reconstruction and Development when such

bond or promissory note is beneficially owned by an individual or a corporation resident in Ceylon.

(4) For the purposes of sub-section (3), the question whether an individual or a corporation is or is not resident in Ceylon shall be determined in accordance with the provisions of section 33 of the Income Tax Ordinance.

(5) Every Guarantee Agreement between the Government and the International Bank for Reconstruction and Development pursuant to this Act and every guarantee given by the Government pursuant to any such Guarantee Agreement shall, notwithstanding anything to the contrary in any law of Ceylon, be valid and enforceable in accordance with their respective terms.

(6) In the case of any loan made to the Corporation by the International Bank for Reconstruction and Development and guaranteed by the Government, the Government shall bear any loss, and be entitled to any profit, resulting from any revaluation of the Ceylon rupee in relation to the currency or currencies in which that loan is expressed.

The amount of every such loss is hereby charged on the Consolidated Fund of Ceylon.

15. The Board of Directors shall cause the accounts of the Corporation to be kept in such form and manner as may be determined by such Board.

16. (1) The accounts of the Corporation shall be audited by two qualified auditors annually appointed at a meeting of the shareholders of the Corporation.

(2) The shareholders shall determine the remuneration of the auditors of the Corporation.

(3) Each auditor of the Corporation shall be supplied with a copy of the annual balance-sheet of the Corporation, and it shall be his duty to examine such balance-sheet together with the accounts and vouchers relating thereto. He shall at all reasonable times have access to the books, accounts and vouchers of the Corporation and shall be entitled to require from the Directors and officers of the Corporation such information and explanations as may be necessary for the performance of his duties.

(4) Each auditor of the Corporation may, if he so desires, make a continuous audit of the accounts of the Corporation.

(5) Each auditor of the Corporation shall make a written report upon the annual balance-sheet and accounts of the Corporation and shall in

such report state whether he has or has not obtained all the information and explanations required by him and whether, in his opinion, such accounts are properly drawn up so as to exhibit a true and correct view of the Corporation's affairs according to the best of his information and the explanations given to him and as shown by the books of the Corporation.

(6) The report of each auditor of the Corporation shall be transmitted by him to the Board of Directors.

(7) The Board of Directors shall cause a copy of the report of each auditor of the Corporation together with a copy of the balance-sheet and profit and loss account to which such report refers to be transmitted to each shareholder and to the Minister of Finance.

17. (1) Every Director, employee or auditor of the Corporation shall, before entering upon his duties, sign a declaration pledging himself to observe strict secrecy respecting all transactions of the Corporation and all matters relating to such transactions, and shall by such declaration pledge himself not to reveal any such transaction or matter except—

(a) when required so to do by the Board of Directors, a court of law, or the person to whom that transaction or matter relates,

(b) in the performance of his duties, and

(c) in order to comply with any of the provisions of this Act or any other law.

(2) Every Director, employee or auditor of the Corporation shall decline to answer any question concerning the business of the Corporation if he cannot answer the question without infringing his pledge of secrecy under sub-section (1).

18. In this Act unless the context otherwise requires—

"agricultural enterprise" means a large scale agricultural or livestock enterprise operated on a commercial basis;

"Board of Directors" means the Board of Directors of the Corporation;

"local authority" means a Municipal Council, an Urban Council, a Town Council, a Village Committee, the Gal Oya Development Board, or any other authority having administrative powers over any area; and

"shareholder" means a shareholder of the Corporation.

APPENDIX D–2

Memorandum of Association of the Pakistan Industrial Credit and Investment Corporation Limited

I. The name of the Company is "THE PAKISTAN INDUSTRIAL CREDIT AND INVESTMENT CORPORATION LIMITED."

II. The Registered Office of the Company will be situated in Karachi.

III. The objects for which the Company is established are:

1. To carry on the business of assisting industrial enterprises within the private sector of industry in Pakistan in general by

(*i*) assisting in the creation, expansion and modernisation of such industrial enterprises;

(*ii*) encouraging, sponsoring and facilitating participation of private capital, internal as well as external, in such enterprises;

(*iii*) encouraging, sponsoring and facilitating private acquisition or ownership of industrial investments, shares and securities;

(*iv*) creating, expanding and stimulating investment, share and security markets;

and in particular by

(a) providing finance in the form of long- or medium-term loans or share participations;

(b) sponsoring and underwriting any issue or conversion of shares and securities;

(c) guaranteeing, and counter-guaranteeing loans and obligations;

(d) making funds available for re-investment by causing the transfer of shares and securities, and by revolving investments, as rapidly as prudent;

(e) furnishing managerial, technical and administrative advice and assisting in obtaining managerial, technical and administrative services to Pakistani industry.

2. (*i*) To buy, underwrite, invest in and acquire and hold shares, stocks, debentures, debenture stock, bonds, obligations and securities issued or guaranteed by any company or body, corporate or unincorporated, or by a person or association.

(*ii*) To acquire any such shares, stocks, debentures, debenture stock, bonds, obligations or securities by original subscription, participation in syndicates, tender, purchase, exchange or otherwise and to subscribe for the same either conditionally or otherwise, and to guarantee the subscription thereof and to exercise and enforce all rights and powers conferred by or incident to the ownership thereof.

(*iii*) To cause, help or aid for remuneration or otherwise the sale, purchase, exchange, transfer or acquisition of shares, stocks, debentures, debenture stock, bonds, obligations or securities.

3. To amalgamate with or enter into partnership or any joint purse or profit-sharing arrangement with or co-operate with or subsidise or assist in any way any company, association or person.

4. To enter into any partnership or arrangement in the nature of a partnership, co-operation or union of interests, with any person or persons, company or association engaged or interested or about to become engaged or interested in the carrying on or conduct of any business or enterprise which this Company is authorised to carry on or conduct or from which this Company would or might derive any benefit, whether direct or indirect.

5. To form, promote, organise and assist or aid in forming promoting, subsidising, organising or aiding companies syndicates or partnerships of all kinds for the purpose of acquiring and undertaking any property and liabilities of this Company or any other Company or of advancing directly or indirectly the objects thereof or for any other purpose which this Company may think expedient and to take or otherwise acquire hold and dispose of shares debentures and other securities in or of any such company and to subsidise or otherwise assist any such company.

6. To enter into arrangements with any State or Authority Central Supreme or State Municipal Local or otherwise which may seem conducive to the Company's objects or any of them and to obtain from any such Government or Authority any concessions grants or decrees rights or privileges whatsoever which the Company may think fit or which may seem to the Company capable of being turned to account and to comply with work develop, carry out, exercise and turn to account any such arrangements concessions grants decrees rights or privileges.

7. To seek for and secure openings for the employment of capital and with the view thereto to prospect, inquire, examine, explore and test and to despatch and employ expeditions, commissions and other agents.

8. To take part in the formation, management, supervision or control of the business or operations of any company or undertaking and for that purpose to render technical and managerial services and act as administrators, managers, secretaries, receivers, managing agents or in any other capacity, and to appoint and remunerate any directors, administrators, managers or accountants or other experts or agents and to share in the remuneration payable to managing agents of such company or undertaking.

9. To form, manage, join or subscribe to any syndicate.

10. To borrow or raise or secure the payment of money by the issue or sale of debentures, debenture stock, bonds, obligations, mortgages and securities of all kinds, either perpetual or terminable and either redeemable or otherwise, and to charge or secure the same by trust deed or otherwise on the undertaking of the Company including its uncalled capital, or upon any specific property and rights, present and future, of the Company or otherwise howsoever.

11. To secure or discharge any debt or obligation of or binding on the Company in such manner as may be thought fit, and in particular by mortgages and charges upon the undertaking and all or any of the assets and property (present and future) and the uncalled capital of the Company or by the creation and issue on such terms as may be thought expedient of debentures, debenture stock, or other securities of any description or by the issue of shares credited as fully or partly paid up.

12. To lend money with or without security and to make advances upon, hold in trust, issue, buy, sell, or otherwise acquire or dispose of, on commission or otherwise, any of the securities or investments of the kinds before mentioned, or to act as agent for any of the above or the like purposes.

13. To facilitate and encourage the creation, issue or conversion of debentures, debenture stock, bonds, obligations, shares, stocks and securities and to act as trustees in connection with any such securities and to take part in the conversion of business concerns and undertakings into companies.

14. To purchase take on lease or in exchange obtain assignments of or otherwise acquire lands and buildings of any tenure or description and any estate or interest in and any rights connected with any lands and buildings convenient for or in connection with its business.

15. To erect construct enlarge alter or maintain buildings and structures of every kind necessary or convenient for the Company's business.

16. To purchase for investment or resale house or other property of

any tenure and any interest therein and to create sell and deal in free-hold and leasehold ground rents and to make advances upon the security of land or house or other property of any interest therein and generally to deal in by way of sale lease exchange or otherwise with land and house property and any other property whether immovable or movable: Provided that such transactions or transaction is connected with an industrial enterprise financed wholly or in part by the Company or is calculated directly or indirectly to develop any branch of the Company's business or to increase the value of or turn to account any of the Company's assets, property or rights.

17. To sell improve manage work develop lease mortgage abandon or in any other manner deal with or dispose of the undertaking of the Company or any part thereof or any part of the property rights and concessions for such consideration as the Company may think fit and in particular for shares debentures and other securities of any other company having objects altogether or in any part similar to those of the Company.

18. To carry on the business of an investment company and to buy underwrite invest in and acquire and hold shares, stocks, debentures, debenture stock, bonds, obligations and securities issued or guaranteed by any company constituted or carrying on business in Pakistan and debentures, debenture stock, bonds, obligations and securities issued or guaranteed by any Government, State, Dominion, Sovereign, Ruler, Commissioners, Public Body or Authority, Supreme, Municipal, Local or otherwise firm or person and to deal with and turn to account the same provided always that no investment imposing unlimited liability on the Company shall be made.

19. To promote organise manage hold dispose of or deal with shares or securities of Unit Trusts whether of fixed or variable character.

20. To act as trustee of any deeds constituting or securing any debentures, debenture stock, or other securities or obligations and to undertake and execute any other trusts, and also to undertake the office of or exercise the powers of executor, administrator, receiver, treasurer, custodian and trust corporation.

21. To constitute any trusts with a view to the issue of preferred and deferred or any other special stocks, securities, certificates or other documents based on or representing any shares, stocks, or other assets appropriated for the purposes of any such trust, and to settle and regulate, and, if thought fit, to undertake and execute any such trusts and to

issue, hold or dispose of any such preferred, deferred, or other special stocks, securities, certificates or documents.

22. To procure the registration or recognition of the Company in or under the laws of any place outside Pakistan.

23. To take such steps as may be necessary to give the Company the same rights and privileges in any part of the world as are possessed by local companies or partnerships of a similar nature.

24. To give guarantees, and carry on and transact every kind of guarantee and counter-guarantee business and in particular to guarantee the payment of any principal moneys, interest or other moneys secured by or payable under any debentures, bonds, debenture stock, mortgages, charges, contracts, obligations and securities, and the payment of dividends on and the repayment of the capital of stocks and shares of all kinds and descriptions.

25. To guarantee and insure the due payment, fulfilment and performance of contracts and obligations of any kind or nature.

26. To undertake and subscribe for, conditionally or unconditionally, stocks, shares and securities of any other company.

27. To appoint trustees (whether individuals or corporations) to hold securities on behalf of and to protect the interests of the Company.

28. To hold in the names of others any property which the Company is authorised to acquire.

29. To carry on any other trade or business whatsoever which can, in the opinion of the Company, be advantageously or conveniently carried on by the Company by way of extension of or in connection with any such business as aforesaid or is calculated directly or indirectly to develop any branch of the Company's business or to increase the value of or turn to account any of the Company's assets, property or rights.

30. To transact or carry on agency business and in particular in relation to the investment of money, the sale of property and the collection and receipt of money.

31. To receive money on time deposit, loan or otherwise, upon such terms as the Company may approve, and to give guarantees and indemnities in respect of the debts and contracts of others.

32. To purchase, or otherwise acquire and undertake, the whole or any part of, or any interest in the business, goodwill, property, contracts, agreements, rights, privileges, effects and liabilities, of any other company, corporation, partnership, body, persons or person carrying on, or having ceased to carry on, any business which the Company is authorised

to carry on, or possessing property suitable for the purposes of the
Company and upon such terms and subject to such stipulations and
conditions and at or for such price or consideration (if any) in money,
shares, moneys' worth, or otherwise as may be deemed advisable.

33. To purchase, take on lease or in exchange, hire or otherwise
acquire any immovable or movable property, patents, licences, rights or
privileges which the Company may think necessary or convenient for
any business of the Company and to develop and turn to account and
deal with the same in such manner as may be thought expedient and
to construct maintain and alter any buildings or works necessary or
convenient for the purposes of the Company.

34. To employ experts to investigate and examine into the condition,
prospects, value, character and circumstances of any business concerns
and undertakings, and generally of any assets, concessions, properties
or rights.

35. To pay for any property or rights acquired by the Company,
either in cash or fully or partly paid shares or by the issue of securities, or partly in one mode and partly in another and generally on
such terms as may be determined.

36. To sell, mortgage, exchange, lease, grant licences, easements, and
other rights over, improve, manage, develop, and turn to account and in
any other manner deal with or dispose of the undertaking, investments,
property, assets, rights and effects of the Company or any part thereof
for such consideration as may be thought fit, including any stocks,
shares or securities of any other company, whether partly or fully paid
up.

37. To draw, make, accept, endorse, discount, negotiate, execute and
issue bills of exchange, promissory notes, and other negotiable or trans-
ferable instruments.

38. To subscribe or guarantee money for any national, charitable,
benevolent, public, general, or useful object or for any exhibition or to
any institution, club, society or fund.

39. To provide for the welfare of employees or ex-employees of the
Company and the wives and families or the dependents or connections
of such persons by building or contributing to the building of houses
or dwellings or by grants of money pensions allowances bonus or
other payments or by creating and from time to time subscribing or
contributing to provident and other associations institutions funds or
trusts and by providing or subscribing or contributing towards places
of instruction and recreation hospitals and dispensaries medical and

other attendance and other assistance as the Company shall think fit.

40. To aid pecuniarily or otherwise, any association, body or movement having for an object the solution, settlement or surmounting of industrial or labour problems or the promotion of industry or trade.

41. To communicate with chambers of commerce, and other mercantile and public bodies in Pakistan and elsewhere, and concert and promote measures for the protection and advancement of trade, industry and commerce and other facilities.

42. To consider, originate and support improvement in the commercial and other laws affecting trade, commerce or manufacture and to promote or oppose legislation and other measures affecting such trade, commerce or manufacture.

43. To undertake and execute any trusts the undertaking whereof may seem desirable and either gratuitously or otherwise.

44. To distribute any of the property or assets of the Company to its members *in specie* or kind.

45. To do all or any of the above things and all such other things as are incidental or as may be thought conducive to the attainment of the above objects or any of them in Pakistan or any other part of the world either as principals, agents, trustees, contractors or otherwise and either alone or in conjunction with others and either by or through agents, contractors, trustees or otherwise and to do all such things as are incidental or conducive to the attainment of the above objects. And it is hereby declared that:

(*i*) the word "company" save when used in reference to this Company in this clause shall be deemed to include any partnership or other body of persons whether incorporated or not incorporated whether domiciled in Pakistan or elsewhere;

(*ii*) the several sub-clauses of this clause and all the powers thereof are to be cumulative and in no case is the generality of any one sub-clause to be narrowed or restricted by any particularity of any other sub-clause nor is any general expression in any sub-clause to be narrowed or restricted by any particularity of expression in the same sub-clause or by the application of any rule of construction *ejusdem generis* or otherwise;

(*iii*) the term "Pakistan" when used in this clause unless repugnant to the context shall include all territories from time to time comprised in the Islamic Republic of Pakistan; and

(*iv*) a nominal share participation in or the loan of money to an industrial enterprise by the Government of Pakistan or of a Province or of a political subdivision of either (whether direct or indirect) shall not by itself be deemed to remove such enterprise from the private sector, so long as such enterprise is privately operated and managed and no such Government has directly or indirectly a controlling interest therein.

IV. The liability of the members is limited.

V. The capital of the Company is Rs. 15,00,00,000 divided into 1,50,00,000 shares of Rs. 10 each with the rights privileges and conditions attached thereto as are provided by the Articles of Association of the Company for the time being with power to increase and reduce the capital of the Company and to divide the shares in the capital for the time being into several classes and to attach thereto respectively such preferential deferred qualified or special rights privileges or conditions as may be determined by or in accordance with the Articles of Association of the Company for the time being and to vary modify or abrogate any such rights privileges or conditions in such manner as may be permitted by the Companies Act, 1913 or provided by the Articles of Association of the Company for the time being.

We, the several persons whose names and addresses are subscribed, are desirous of being formed into a company in pursuance to this Memorandum of Association and we respectively agree to take the number of shares in the capital of the Company set opposite our respective names.

Names, addresses and descriptions   Number of shares taken by each
     of subscribers.   subscriber.

Abstract of Articles of Association of The Pakistan Industrial Credit and Investment Corporation Ltd.

Table A Excluded

CALLS

Text of Selected Articles

Borrowing Powers

69. Subject to the provisions of these presents the Directors may from time to time at their discretion borrow any sum or sums of money for the purposes of the Company: Provided that the Directors shall not, subject to any restrictions imposed by the terms of the Agreements mentioned in Article 4(1)(a) and (b), borrow or guarantee any sum of money which after such borrowing or guarantee will make the amount borrowed and guaranteed by the Company and at that date outstanding (including that portion only of the Government advance which pursuant to the Agreement referred to in Article 4(1)(a) shall

at that date have become due for payment) exceed an amount equal to three times the aggregate of (1) the unimpaired capital of the Company, (2) the amount of the Government advance at the time outstanding but not yet due for payment, and (3) the surplus and reserves of the Company: Provided, however, that the rights of any lender or other person dealing with the Company shall not be affected by the transgression of these limits. For the purpose of this Article the amounts of the unimpaired capital and of the surplus and reserves of the Company shall be those ascertained and certified by the Company's auditors on the basis that the Company is a going concern: Provided that such a certification shall be deemed to be valid for a period of six months from its date.

Directors

115. (1) Until otherwise determined by a General Meeting the number of Directors shall be not less than 5 or more than 15 including the Government Director and the Appointed Directors (if any) but excluding the Debenture Director (if any).

(2) (a) During such time as not less than 2,00,000 Ordinary Shares or 7 per cent of the paid-up ordinary capital (whichever is the greater) is held by shareholders whose principal residence or head office is in the United Kingdom or who being Insurance Companies are members of the British Insurance Association, and who notify the Company in writing of their intention to be included within the group of shareholders to whom this sub-clause shall apply, such person or company as shall from time to time be designated in a writing signed by the holders of a majority of the shares held at the time by such shareholders and filed in the Office, shall have the right from time to time to appoint one person as a Director of the Company and to remove such person from office and on a vacancy being caused in such office from any cause whether by resignation, death, removal or otherwise to appoint a Director in the vacant place.

(b) During such time as not less than 2,00,000 Ordinary Shares or 7 per cent of the paid-up ordinary capital (whichever is the greater) is held by shareholders whose principal residence or head office is in Japan, and who notify the Company in writing of their intention to be included within the group of shareholders to whom this sub-clause shall apply, such person or company as shall from time to time be designated in a writing signed by the holders of a majority of the shares held at the time by such shareholders and filed in the Office, shall have the right from time to time to appoint one person as a Director of the Company and to remove such person from office and on a vacancy being caused in such office from any cause whether by resignation, death, removal or otherwise to appoint a Director in the vacant place.

(c) During such time as not less than 2,00,000 Ordinary Shares or 7 per cent of the ordinary paid-up capital (whichever is the greater) is held by shareholders whose principal residence or head office is in the United States or Canada, and who notify the Company in writing of their intention to be included within the group of shareholders to whom this sub-clause shall apply, such person or company as shall from time to time be designated in a writing signed by the holders of a majority of the shares held at the time by such shareholders and filed in the Office, shall have the right from time to time to appoint one person as a Director of the Company and to remove such person from office and on a vacancy being caused in such office from any cause whether by resignation, death, removal or otherwise to appoint a Director in the vacant place.

(d) The Directors appointed under sub-clauses (a), (b), or (c) above are herein referred to as the "Appointed Directors" and the term "Appointed Directors" means the Directors for the time being in office under the provisions of sub-clauses (a), (b), or (c) above or any of them. The Appointed Directors shall not be liable to retire by rotation and shall not be bound to hold any qualification shares. Subject as aforesaid the Appointed Directors shall be entitled to the same rights and privileges and be subject to the same obligations as any other Director of the Company.

(e) No shareholder may be included within more than one of the groups of shareholders referred to in subclauses (a), (b), and (c) above.

117. During such time as any amount of the Government advance shall remain unpaid, the President of Pakistan shall have the right from time to time to appoint one person as a Director of the Company and to remove such person from office and on a vacancy being caused in such office from any cause whether by resignation, death, removal or otherwise to appoint a Director in the vacant place. The Director appointed under this Article is in these presents referred to as the "Government Director" and the term "Government Director" means

the Director for the time being in office under this Article. The Government Director shall not be liable to retire by rotation or be removed from office except by the President of Pakistan as aforesaid. The Government Director shall not be bound to hold any qualification shares. Subject as aforesaid the Government Director shall be entitled to the same rights and privileges and be subject to the same obligations as any other Director of the Company.

127. Subject to the restrictions imposed by these presents and the Act and the observance and fulfilment thereof, no Director shall be disqualified by his office from contracting with the Company either as a vendor, purchaser, agent, broker or otherwise, nor shall any such contract, or any contract or arrangement entered into by or on behalf of the Company in which any Director shall be in any way interested be avoided nor shall any Director, so contracting or being so interested be liable to account to the Company for any profit realised by any such contract or arrangement by reason only of such Director holding that office, or of the fiduciary relation thereby established, but it is declared that the nature of his interest must be disclosed by him at the meeting of the Directors at which the contract or arrangement is determined on, if his interest then exists or in any other case at the first meeting of the Directors after the acquisition of his interest, and that no Director shall, as a Director, vote in respect of any contract or arrangement in which he is so interested, and if he does so vote his vote shall not be counted: Provided that the Directors, or any of them, may vote on any contract of indemnity against any loss which they or any one or more of them may suffer by reason of becoming or being sureties or a surety for the Company. A general notice that any Director is a member of any specified firm or a Director or member of any specified company and is to be regarded as interested in any subsequent transaction with such firm or company, shall be sufficient disclosure under this Article, and after such general notice it shall not be necessary to give any special notice relating to any particular transaction with such firm or company.

APPENDIX D–3

Memorandum of Association of Industrial and Mining Development Bank of Iran

ARTICLE I

Name

The name of the corporation is "INDUSTRIAL AND MINING DEVELOPMENT BANK OF IRAN."

ARTICLE II

Offices

The registered office of the corporation will be situated at Tehran, Iran. The corporation may have such branches in Iran and in foreign countries as the Board of Directors may from time to time determine.

ARTICLE III

Duration

The corporation shall have unlimited duration.

ARTICLE IV

Objects

The objects for which the corporation is established are to develop, encourage and stimulate private industrial, productive, mining and transportation enterprises in Iran, in general by:

(i) assisting in the creation, expansion, and modernization of such enterprises;

(ii) encouraging, sponsoring and facilitating participation of private capital, internal as well as external, in such enterprises; and

(iii) creating, expanding and stimulating public investment and security markets; and in particular by:

(a) Financing in the form of long or medium term loan or participations in the share capital of other companies;

(b) sponsoring and underwriting the issue of all forms of shares and securities;

(c) guaranteeing, and counter-guaranteeing, loans and commitments;

(d) making funds available for re-investment by causing the transfer and sale of shares and securities;

(e) offering necessary guidance to Iranian industry in technical, financial, managerial and administrative matters; and

(f) encouraging and sponsoring technical, financial, managerial and administrative knowledge in the country.

The fact that the Government of Iran or any agency or instrumentality thereof shall have an interest in any enterprise shall not result in such enterprise being other than private for the purposes of the foregoing objects so long as such enterprise is privately operated and managed and the Government or any agency or instrumentality thereof does not have a controlling interest therein.

ARTICLE V

Powers

The corporation shall have and exercise, in general, all such powers as may be necessary for or conducive or incidental to the attainment of any of the objects herein expressed, and, in particular, without limiting the generality of the foregoing, the powers:

(1) To lend money and negotiate loans in Iranian money and foreign moneys, whether secured or unsecured; to guarantee in whole or in part the payment of money or the performance of any obligation or undertaking.

(2) To acquire, sell, negotiate, guarantee, deal in, mortgage, pledge or otherwise dispose of, all forms of securities; to do any acts and things designed to protect or enhance the value of any securities; and, while the owner or holder of any securities, or any interest therein, to possess and to exercise in respect thereof all the rights, powers and privileges incident to such ownership, title or interest.

(3) To act as underwriter or broker; and generally to carry on the business of buying and selling and dealing in securities, commodities and other property and interests of any kind; and to act as financial, commercial or general agent or representative and as such to develop, improve and extend the property, trade and business interests of others.

(4) To conduct researches, investigations and technical studies in

respect of securities, organizations, businesses and general business conditions; to establish and operate pilot plants; to secure information pertinent to the investment and the improvement of the assets and funds of the corporation and of others; to furnish statistical data, advisory service and investment advice; to manage investments and funds for the Government of Iran or any agency or instrumentality thereof; and to procure any or all of the foregoing to be performed by others as independent contractors and to pay compensation therefor.

(5) To purchase, lease, or otherwise acquire, hold, manage, sell, transfer, mortgage, pledge or otherwise encumber or dispose of foreign exchange, coin and bullion and any and all goods, wares, merchandise, commodities and other property, real, personal or mixed of every kind and description, wheresoever situated or located, necessary or appropriate for any of the objects or powers herein expressed.

(6) To purchase or otherwise acquire the whole or any part of the property, goodwill, rights, business and franchises, and to take over as a going concern the whole or any part of the assets and liabilities of any individual, partnership, association, company or corporation, and to hold or in any manner dispose of the whole or any part of the property so acquired, and to continue and conduct the whole or any part of the business acquired and exercise all powers necessary or convenient to the conduct and management of such business.

(7) To acquire, hold, use, develop, sell, assign or otherwise dispose of, any and all licenses, permits, franchises, concessions, lands, patents, patent rights, copyrights, trademarks, trade names, and similar rights.

(8) To borrow money and otherwise contract indebtedness in Iran and foreign countries and in Iranian money or foreign moneys; to draw, make, accept, endorse, execute and issue and sell or otherwise dispose of notes, drafts, bills of exchange, warrants, bonds and other evidences of indebtedness, for moneys borrowed or in payment of any and all property purchased or acquired, or to effect any of the objects of the corporation; to secure the same by mortgage, conveyance, deed of trust or pledge of, or by other lien or charge upon, any or all of the property, franchises, rights and privileges of every kind, wheresoever situated, then owned or thereafter acquired by the corporation; to confer upon the holders of bonds or other obligations of the corporation, secured or unsecured, and either before or after the issuance thereof, the right to convert the same into stock of the corporation upon such terms and conditions as may be deemed advisable.

ARTICLE VI

Share Capital

(1) The initial capital of the corporation is Rials 400,000,000 divided into 400,000 shares of the value of Rials 1,000 each.

(2) *Classes of Shares:* The share capital of the corporation is divided into two classes:

Class A which shall always represent not less than 60% of the total capital of the corporation and shall be subscribed to exclusively by nationals of Iran.

Class B which shall represent the balance of the shares and may be subscribed to by nationals of nations other than Iran.

All shares of Class A shall at all times be owned by Iranian nationals and may not be transferred to non-Iranian nationals.

(3) *Registration:* There shall be kept at the registered office of the corporation a book, to be known as the stock book, containing the names of all persons who are shareholders, showing their addresses and the number of shares of each class held by them and the time when they become the owners thereof. The corporation shall be entitled to treat the holder of record of any share as the owner thereof.

ARTICLE VII

Amendment Limitations

The corporation reserves the right to amend, alter, change or repeal any provision contained in this Memorandum of Association in any manner now or hereafter permitted by the laws of Iran. However, no amendment, alteration, change or repeal shall be made without the affirmative vote of the holders of a majority of the shares of each class of shares of the corporation given at a special assembly called for the purpose, at which the holders of at least three-fourths of all shares shall be present or represented.

We, the several persons whose names and addresses are subscribed, are desirous of being formed into a corporation in pursuance of the Memorandum of Association, and we respectfully agree to take the number of shares in the capital of the corporation set opposite our respective names:

Names, addresses and description   Number of shares taken by each
      of subscribers.   subscriber.

Dated: The .... day of .... 1959.

Articles of Association of Industrial and Mining Development Bank of Iran

PRELIMINARY

These Articles of Association in addition to matters contained in the Memorandum of Association of the Corporation hereinafter provide the rules and regulations by which the Corporation is to be managed and its business to be carried out and transacted.

ARTICLE I

A. RIGHTS AND RESPONSIBILITIES OF SHAREHOLDERS

1. Each holder of common stock shall be entitled to one vote for each share held by him.

2. The responsibilities of the shareholders are limited to the shares owned by them.

3. In case the Corporation's capital is increased and new shares are issued, shareholders of common stock of Class A shall have priority to purchase new Class A shares pro-rata to the shares owned by them, and shareholders of common stock of Class B shall have priority to purchase new Class B shares pro-rata to the shares owned by them.

4. Any action which under the Law or under these Articles would require the affirmative vote of shareholders at a meeting called for the purpose, shall require the affirmative vote of a majority of the shares of each class of the common shares of the corporation, at such meeting or any subsequent meeting or adjournment thereof.

B. CERTIFICATES

Certificates representing shares shall be registered and in such form as shall be authorized by the Board of Directors. Certificates for the Class A shares shall contain appropriate provisions sufficient to put the holder on notice of the restriction with respect to the Iranian nationality of the holders of shares of such class. Such certificates shall be signed by the Managing Director or the Associate Managing Director and by the Secretary or an Assistant Secretary. All certificates for shares shall be consecutively numbered.

C. INCREASE OF SHARE CAPITAL

The directors may, with the sanction of a special resolution of the shareholders, increase the capital by creation of new shares, such aggregate increase to be of such amount and to be divided into shares of such respective amounts as the resolution shall prescribe.

D. FORFEITURE

In connection with any offering of any shares of stock of the Corporation, failure by any subscriber to pay any amount due on shares subscribed for will render such shares and previous payments in respect thereof liable to forfeiture provided that in connection with any forfeiture the Corporation shall proceed in accordance with the applicable provisions of the Law of Commerce.

ARTICLE II

Shareholders Assemblies

A. INITIAL ASSEMBLY

An initial assembly of shareholders shall be held as soon as convenient after all capital stock of the corporation is subscribed and one-half thereof paid in cash. Such assembly shall elect the first directors and inspectors of the Corporation, approve the Articles of Association and take all such other action as may be appropriate to complete the formation of the Corporation.

B. GENERAL ASSEMBLY

A general assembly of the shareholders shall be held at such place as the Board of Directors may from time to time determine, not later than the end of the month of Tir (July 23) in each year beginning with the first full fiscal year after the date of the initial assembly, for the purposes of electing directors, approving financial statements and the report of the Inspectors and the transaction of such other business as may come before the assembly.

C. SPECIAL ASSEMBLIES

Special assemblies of the shareholders may be called by the Board of Directors at any time and shall be called by the Board of Directors at the written request of the Inspectors or of the holders of not less than one-fifth of all the outstanding shares entitled to vote at such assembly.

D. NOTICE

Written notice stating the date, time and place of the assembly, and, in case of a special assembly, the purposes for which the assembly is called, shall be transmitted by the most expeditious method to insure delivery not less than thirty nor more than forty days before the date of such assembly, to each shareholder of record entitled to vote at such assembly.

E. RECORD DATE

The date on which notice of any assembly is transmitted shall be the record date for the determination of the shareholders entitled to notice of and to vote at such assembly or any adjournment thereof.

F. PROXIES

At an assembly a shareholder may vote either in person or by proxy executed by an instrument in writing by the shareholder or by his duly authorized attorney-in-fact.

G. QUORUM

Each shareholder of record may attend and vote at any assembly. Except as otherwise provided by the Law of Commerce or these Articles of Association, the holders of record of a majority of the outstanding shares of each class entitled to vote present in person or represented by proxy, shall constitute a quorum for an assembly. If less than a majority of each class of stock is represented at an assembly, such number may adjourn the assembly in accordance with the provisions of the Law of Commerce. At an adjourned assembly at which a quorum of one-third of each class of stock shall be present or represented, any business may be transacted which might have been transacted at the assembly as originally notified.

H. VOTING

Shares of its own stock belonging to the Corporation shall not be voted. Except as otherwise provided by the Law of Commerce or these Articles of Association, each matter which shall properly come before any assembly shall be decided by the vote of shareholders entitled to cast a majority of the votes of each class of shares, a quorum being present. All elections of directors shall be held by ballot. If the Chairman of the assembly shall so determine or any shareholder shall so request, a vote shall be taken by ballot on any other matter.

ARTICLE III

Board of Directors and Executive Committee

A. NUMBER AND ELECTION

The Corporation shall be managed by a Board of Directors. The Board of Directors shall have the entire management of the affairs of the Corporation and is vested with all the powers possessed by the Corporation itself so far as this delegation of authority is not inconsistent with the Law or these Articles.

The Board shall consist of fifteen directors. The holders of Class A shares shall have the right, by the vote of a majority in number of the shares of such class, to elect seven directors during the period of five years commencing with the date of the initial assembly, and thereafter to elect eight directors. The holders of Class B shares shall have the right, by the vote of a majority in number of the shares of such class, to elect eight directors during the initial five year period, and thereafter to elect seven directors. After the expiration of five years from the date of the initial meeting of shareholders any shares of Class B then owned or thereafter acquired by nationals of Iran shall be surrendered to the Corporation for cancellation and exchange into an equal number of shares of Class A and for each aggregate of 22,000 Class B shares so surrendered and exchanged into Class A shares the number of directors to be elected by the holders of Class A shares shall be increased by one and the number of directors to be elected by the holders of Class B shares shall be decreased by one.

B. GOVERNMENT OBSERVER

In the event that the Government of Iran shall have the right to appoint an observer pursuant to the terms of any agreement between the Government of Iran and the corporation, such observer may be appointed by the Government of Iran to attend all Board Meetings of the Directors as well as all assemblies of the corporation and all meetings of the Executive Committee, but he shall not be entitled to vote at any such meetings.

Such observer would be entitled to receive such information as he might be entitled to receive if he were a Director and the Directors of the corporation are bound to furnish him such information. He might be removed and his successor appointed by the Iranian Government at pleasure.

C. TENURE AND QUALIFICATIONS

Each director elected by shareholders shall hold office until the next general assembly and until his successor shall have been elected and qualified. Any person owning ten or more shares shall be qualified to be a director. Such ten qualifying shares shall be deposited with the corporation.

D. ALTERNATE DIRECTORS

Each director may appoint an alternate who, in the absence of the said director, may perform all duties which the said director might perform. An alternate director may be removed either with or without cause by the director by whom he was appointed, upon notice of such removal to the Secretary of the Board.

E. REGULAR MEETINGS

A regular meeting of the Board of Directors shall be held without notice immediately after the general assembly. The Board may provide by resolution for the holding of additional regular meetings without other notice than such resolution.

F. SPECIAL MEETINGS

Special meetings of the Board of Directors may be called by any director elected by holders of Class A shares and any director elected by holders of Class B shares, acting jointly. The directors calling any such meeting shall give twenty days' written and telegraphic notice stating the purposes of such meeting.

G. QUORUM AND MANNER OF ACTING

A majority of the directors shall constitute a quorum for any meeting of the Board of Directors, provided, however, that during the period of 5 years following the initial assembly of shareholders such majority shall include at least two directors elected by the holders of Class A shares and at least two directors elected by the holders of Class B shares, and any Board action, to be valid, must receive the affirmative vote of the majority of the Directors present elected by the holders of Class B shares. The act of a majority of the directors present may adjourn the meeting from time to time, and no notice of such adjourned meeting need be given.

H. SIGNED RESOLUTION

A resolution signed by all the directors shall be as valid and effective as if it had been passed at a meeting of the Board.

I. RESIGNATION, REMOVAL AND VACANCIES

Any director may resign at any time by giving written notice to the Chairman of the Board. Any director elected by shareholders may be removed, either with or without cause, at any time by the vote of the holders of a majority of the shares of the class by which such director was elected, at a special assembly of the holders of such shares called for the purpose. Upon the death, resignation or removal of any director elected by shareholders, the resulting vacancy may be filled by the vote of the remaining directors who shall have been elected by holders of shares of the class by which such director was elected. A director elected to fill a vacancy shall be elected for the unexpired term of his predecessor.

J. COMPENSATION

Directors and their alternates shall be entitled to reasonable directors' attendance fees and reimbursement for reasonable expenses incurred in the exercise of their duties. The remuneration of the Directors may from time to time be determined by a resolution at a general meeting. No director or alternate shall be precluded from serving the corporation in any other capacity and receiving compensation therefor when duly approved by the Board of Directors.

K. DISCLOSURE OF INTEREST

If any director or alternate shall have any personal interest, direct or indirect, in any transaction in which the corporation proposes to engage, he shall disclose such fact to the Board of Directors and the interested director or alternate shall not vote thereon.

L. EXECUTIVE COMMITTEE

1. The Board of Directors shall appoint from their number an Executive Committee consisting of five members. During the period of five years from the date of the initial assembly two of the members of the Executive Committee shall be directors elected by the holders of Class A shares and three of the members shall be directors elected by the holders of Class B shares, and thereafter three of the members shall be directors elected by the holders of Class A shares and two of the members shall be directors elected by the holders of Class B shares. Each member of the Executive Committee may from time to time in his discretion appoint and remove an alternate who, in the absence of the member shall have the same powers and may perform all duties which the member might perform. The member shall be responsible to the corporation for all acts or omissions of the alternate. The Executive Committee shall have and may exercise all the powers of the Board of

Directors (except the power to appoint or remove a member of the Executive Committee, the power to fill vacancies in the Board and the power to remove an officer appointed by the Board) when the Board is not in session. Any member of the Executive Committee may be removed (either with or without cause) at any time by resolution of the Board. During the period of five years, commencing with the initial assembly any action of the Executive Committee, to be valid, must receive the affirmative vote of the majority of the members present who shall have been appointed by the Directors elected by the holders of Class B shares.

2. The Executive Committee shall meet from time to time on call of any member who is a director elected by holders of Class A shares and any member who is a director elected by holders of Class B shares, acting jointly. The Executive Committee shall also meet from time to time on call of the Managing Director.

ARTICLE IV

Officers

A. NUMBER AND ELECTION

The officers of the corporation shall consist of a Chairman of the Board, a Managing Director, an Associate Managing Director, a Secretary and a Treasurer and such other officers as the Board of Directors or the Executive Committee may from time to time determine. They shall be elected from time to time by the Board of Directors for such period or periods as the Board may determine.

B. RESIGNATION, REMOVAL AND VACANCIES

Any officer may resign by giving written notice to the Board of Directors. The acceptance of such resignation shall not be necessary to make it effective. Any officer or agent elected by the Board of Directors may be removed by the Board.

C. CHAIRMAN OF THE BOARD

A Chairman of the Board of Directors shall be chosen by the Board voting without regard to class from among its members elected by the holders of Class A shares. The Chairman shall preside at all meetings of the Board and at the assemblies of shareholders. In the absence of the Chairman of the Board, an acting chairman may be elected by majority vote.

D. MANAGING DIRECTOR AND ASSOCIATE MANAGING DIRECTOR

The Managing Director shall be the principal executive officer of the corporation, and, subject to the control of the Board, shall have general supervision of the business of the corporation and of its officers. The Managing Director shall exercise such powers as from time to time are entrusted to and conferred upon him by the Board of Directors. The Managing Director shall have the right to receive notice of and to attend and participate in all meetings of the Board of Directors and the Executive Committee and any other committee appointed by the Board, but shall not have the right to vote at any such meeting unless he be a director or member of the committee. The Associate Managing Director shall perform the duties of the Managing Director in his absence.

E. SECRETARY AND TREASURER

The Secretary shall be responsible for the keeping of the minutes of all meetings and assemblies, the giving of all notices in accordance with these Articles or as required by law, the safekeeping of the records and the seal of the corporation and the affixing thereof when duly authorized, the execution individually or with such other officer as may be designated of all documents and transactions of the corporation so authorized by the Board of Directors, have general charge of the stock book of the corporation and in general perform all duties incident to the office of Secretary and such other duties as from time to time may be assigned by the Managing Director or by the Board of Directors.

The Treasurer shall have charge and custody of and be responsible for all funds and securities of the corporation, receive and give receipts for moneys due and payable to the corporation from any source whatsoever, deposit all such funds and securities in the name of the corporation in such banks or other depositaries as shall be selected in accordance with these Articles, make payment of amounts properly payable by the Corporation, supervise the keeping of all financial records and perform such other duties as from time to time may be assigned by the

Managing Director or by the Board of Directors. If required by the Board of Directors, the Treasurer shall give bond for the faithful discharge of his duties in such sum and with such surety or sureties as the Board of Directors shall determine.

F. SALARIES

The salaries of the officers shall be fixed by the Board of Directors.

ARTICLE V

Contracts and Financial Transactions

A. CONTRACTS

The Board of Directors may authorize any officer or officers, or agent or agents, to enter into contracts or sign, execute and deliver instruments or deeds in the name and on behalf of the corporation.

B. BORROWING

No borrowing shall be contracted on behalf of the corporation unless authorized by a resolution of the Board of Directors.

ARTICLE VI

Inspectors

The shareholders shall, at the initial assembly and at each general assembly, by majority vote, elect two Inspectors to serve for a one year term. One Inspector shall be elected by the holders of Class A shares and the other shall be elected by the holders of Class B shares. The authority, powers and duties of the Inspectors shall be as provided by the Law of Commerce.

ARTICLE VII

Fiscal Matters

A. FISCAL YEAR

The fiscal year of the corporation shall commence on the first day of Farvardin and end on the last day of Esfand in each year.

B. STATEMENTS AND REPORTS

In addition to any statutory provision for the publication of any summaries of accounts, the Board of Directors shall submit a balance sheet every six months to the Inspectors. The Board shall also submit to the Inspectors for submission to each general assembly of shareholders, at least thirty days before the meeting of such an assembly, a balance sheet as of the end of the preceding fiscal year and a statement of profit and loss for such year certified by professionally qualified accountants independent of the corporation to be appointed annually by the Board of Directors. A copy of each annual balance sheet and statement of profit and loss together with the report of the Inspectors shall be mailed to each Iranian shareholder not less than fifteen days before the general assembly and airmailed to non-Iranian shareholders not less than 20 days before the general assembly.

C. DIVIDENDS

The Board of Directors may recommend for payment, and, if approved by the shareholders at the next general assembly, the corporation may pay, out of its accumulated net profits as herein defined, dividends on outstanding shares. For the purposes of this paragraph the term "net profit" shall mean the excess of (a) the gross income of the corporation computed in accordance with sound accounting principles over (b) the sum of all proper expenses and charges, provision for all taxes, and such reserves as may be established by the Board all in accordance with sound accounting principles, or as may be required by law.

ARTICLE VIII

Amendments, Dissolution

Subject to the next succeeding paragraph of this Article, and except as otherwise provided by the Law of Commerce, these Articles of Association may be amended by the shareholders at a special assembly called for the purpose, by vote of a majority of the shareholders present or represented, provided that the holders of at least three-fourths of all shares of the corporation are present or represented.

No amendment of paragraph (A) of Article I, or of paragraphs (G) and (H) of Article II, or of Article III, shall be made nor shall the Corporation be dissolved without the affirmative vote of the holders of a majority of the shares of each class at a special assembly called for the purpose at which the holders of at least two-thirds of the shares of each class shall be present or represented.

Appraisal of Proposals and Supervision of Investments

Industrial Credit and Investment Corporation of India

20th April, 1959.

Appraisal and Presentation of Proposals

1. This instruction lays out the system of appraisal and presentation that will henceforth be used for all applications made to the ICICI.

2. Immediately upon receipt of an application, the usual one-page "As Received" summary will be prepared for the Board. It will be drawn up by the staff member to whom Mr. ——— assigns it.

3. The proposal will then be studied by the Project Analysis Department. That study will be based on the contents of the application itself, on discussions with the applicant, on a visit to the site (where that is relevant) and on *independent inquiries* by the staff. The latter is of particular importance in considering the market the applicant proposes to serve and the technical processes he intends to use.

4. A check-list of the data that should be gathered and examined by the staff is attached. The check-list is a guide to the staff; it will *not* be given to applicants. No such check-list can be comprehensive and not every item in it will be relevant to every application. It will be up to the staff to adapt its investigation to the particular case in hand.

5. When the staff's study has been completed, a *brief but comprehen-*

189

sive appraisal of the proposal will be prepared. This appraisal must be prepared jointly by an engineer and by a financial analyst, one of whom will be the person to whom Mr. ———— originally assigned the application (in 2 above). The appraisal will set forth the salient features of the proposal as it has emerged from the discussions with the applicant, a critical analysis of it, and the staff's recommendation. The appraisal should be drafted in accordance with the outline appended to this instruction, adapted as circumstances require. On completion, it is to be submitted to the General Manager.

6. When this appraisal has been discussed with, revised (if necessary) and approved by the General Manager, the staff member to whom it was originally assigned will proceed to draft the General Manager's condensed personal statement and recommendation to the Board. That statement will follow the same outline (with only such appendices as may be necessary) as the appraisal itself, will be written in the first person singular and will be headed as follows:—

MEMORANDUM FROM THE GENERAL MANAGER

Appraisal of   Proposal

The statement will set forth only essential details and will concentrate on evaluation and recommendations.

7. There will be no "Supplementary Memoranda" to the Board unless, after it has accepted or rejected a proposal, it becomes necessary to reopen the case or unless the Board asks for additional study of a proposal. When an agreement has been signed concerning a proposal already sanctioned by the Board, a memorandum will be presented to the Board informing it of the action taken.

8. The staff member to whom the application was originally assigned will continue, after the investment has been made, to maintain a watching brief over it.

9. The staff appraisal referred to in 5 above, suitably revised, will henceforth be submitted to the IBRD in support of a request for approval of a foreign exchange loan. To this appraisal will be added a short note covering the following items:—

a) Action taken by the Board;
b) Terms of proposed loan, including Amortization Schedule;
c) Security to be taken;
d) Foreign exchange requirements by currencies, quarterly;

e) List of goods to be financed by IBRD;
f) Special features of proposed loan contract, (including special arrangements for supervision, if any, and special covenants).

Appraisal of .... *Proposal*

A one-paragraph statement setting forth the names of the promoters, or applicants, the nature of the proposal and what is required of the ICICI.

A. THE PROMOTERS (including who they are, their reputation, their worth and what they intend to do).

B. THE PROJECT (including the main facts of the proposal, its requirements of labor, essential services and raw materials, sources of equipment, technical collaboration, schedule for carrying out main items in construction of project, e.g., placement of orders, preparation of land, erection of buildings, delivery of equipment, installation of equipment).

C. THE COST OF THE PROJECT (estimates of cost including requirements of working capital, a judgment of their reasonableness).

D. MEANS OF FINANCING (sources of finance, their reasonableness, what is required from the ICICI, security in the event of loan).

E. THE MARKET (including supply and demand for the product present and prospective, expected rate of growth of consumption, domestic production and imports, import and excise duties, competitive enterprises, main buyers, if any, prevailing and expected prices, machinery for distribution).

F. PROFITABILITY (including unit production costs, selling prices, profits, taxation, cash availability to meet obligations, expected return on investment, operating ratios, break-even point).

G. MANAGEMENT (who will direct construction and operation, their experience, their capacity to do the job).

H. STATUS OF GOVERNMENT CONSENTS (what has been done and what remains to be done).

I. RECOMMENDATIONS (whether the ICICI should reject or approve the proposal, in the latter case on what terms, what special conditions if any should be imposed).

Appendices:

Comparative balance sheets and profit and loss statements
Detailed estimate of capital cost

Detailed estimate of cost of production and profit
Income and cash flow during construction and first years of operation
Pro-forma balance sheets at start of operation and on attainment of
    normal production
Technical reports
Any other

Signatures . . . .

. . . .

. . . .

Date: . . . .

20th April, 1959.

Follow-up of ICICI Investments

1. An essential part of ICICI's work is the follow-up and supervision
of its investments. Provision for reporting and inspection is made in the
Heads of Agreement in the case of all loans, both of rupees and of
foreign exchange. Consideration is being given to whether similar provisions can be made in other types of investment. In the meantime, the
following applies only to loans.

2. Since ICICI is equally concerned with the success of projects involving rupee loans and of projects involving foreign exchange, precisely the same provisions concerning supervision will be made in all
cases of loans. The provisions now used in foreign exchange loans (except references to IBRD) are to be used in rupee loans as well.

3. The object of ICICI's follow-up policy is (a) to determine, during
the period of construction, whether the project will be completed on
schedule and within the financial resources available; (b) to determine,

during operation, how sales and profits compare with the original expectations; and (c) to find, as early as possible, whether circumstances have impeded or threaten to impede the realization of targets and expectations and, if so, what remedial action to take. In pursuit of this policy, regular reports are to be required from all clients and regular inspections are to be made by staff, the results of both of which are to be reported to the General Manager.

4. REPORTING ON PROJECTS:

a) Two types of reports are to be required: during the period of construction, reports on physical and financial progress; and during both construction and operation, production and sales in quantities and balance sheets and profit and loss accounts. These reports are to be submitted within six weeks of the reporting period.

b) During negotiation of the loan, ICICI and client must agree on schedules of construction and of expenditure.

c) The standard form of reports and charts is given in the attachment. It is to be modified as necessary for each individual case. The form of report and the form of charts to be used to illustrate it are to be given to the client immediately on conclusion of Heads of Agreement.

d) On receipt of each report, a brief summary will be given to the General Manager, calling attention to departures from plan and to special problems and indicating what, if any, action ought to be taken by ICICI.

5. INSPECTION OF PROJECTS:

a) At least one inspection of every project is to be made each year.

b) In the case of projects presenting difficulties, at least two inspections are to be made each year.

c) Immediately after each inspection, a report is to be given to the General Manager. That report should cover the following points:—

1) Concise statement of the position and condition of project, with particular reference to relation to original financial and physical targets.

2) Details of and reasons for any departure from original targets.

3) Determination of whether funds provided were used for purposes for which intended.

4) Compliance with special provisions of Heads of Agreement.

5) Major developments which might affect construction or operation.

6) Action, if any, required by ICICI.

6. RESPONSIBILITY:

a) Mr. —— has the responsibility for keeping a card index of the due dates and arrival dates of all reports. This must be kept up-to-date at all times. To this end, all reports must be registered on his index as soon as they arrive. If the due date goes by without receipt of the report due, it is his responsibility immediately to inform Mr. —— so that a reminder may be sent without delay. If there is no response, the matter is to be called to the attention of the General Manager.

b) Mr. —— has the responsibility for presenting the staff reports referred to in 4 (d) and 5 (c) above to the General Manager, no matter who does the drafting or the inspection.

c) Mr. —— also has the responsibility for scheduling the inspections called for in 5 (a) and (b) above. To the extent possible, such inspections will be made to coincide with other staff travel; but the effort to conserve travel will not be permitted to interfere with the regularity of inspections. The staff member assigned an inspection will, before going, consult with Mr. ——, (and if necessary with the General Manager) in order to lay out a precise agenda for his inspection.

General Manager.

Standard Reports and Charts

ENGINEERING & CONSTRUCTION (Quarterly during construction):

1. Progress in the preparation of final plans, designs and specifications.

2. Progress in placing of contracts and orders for services and equipment, and progress made in the manufacture and delivery of the equipment.

3. Progress in the physical construction of the project, and installation of the equipment.

4. Progress of plans for the training of men who will operate the plant when it goes into production.

FINANCIAL (Quarterly during construction):

5. Position of project funds, showing how much has been spent, how much is required to complete the project, and whether the available resources are sufficient.

6. Major revisions in financing plans of the project (cash flow estimate).

OPERATIONS:

7. At the end of construction, a final report on the project including a physical description of the project as completed, together with a statement of its final cost and sources of financing, indicating all major changes from the original plans and cost estimates.

8. Reports on physical production and sales and copies of Balance Sheets and Profit & Loss Accounts. (Semi-annually during construction and operation; in the case of new enterprises, production and sales reports cannot begin until construction is completed.)

OTHER:

9. Reasons for differences between plans and progress.

10. Any major developments which threaten to affect the normal progress of construction or operation.

11. Such other items as may be desirable in the particular circumstances.

Index

197